The
Full-Time Faculty
HANDBOOK

The
Full-Time Faculty
HANDBOOK

Edited by
Virginia Bianco-Mathis
Neal Chalofsky

SAGE Publications
International Educational and Professional Publisher
Thousand Oaks London New Delhi

For information:

 SAGE Publications, Inc.
2455 Teller Road
Thousand Oaks, California 91320
E-mail: order@sagepub.com

SAGE Publications Ltd.
6 Bonhill Street
London EC2A 4PU
United Kingdom

SAGE Publications India Pvt. Ltd.
M-32 Market
Greater Kailash I
New Delhi 110 048 India

Printed in the United States of America

Library of Congress Cataloging-in-Publication Data

Main entry under title:

The full-time faculty handbook / edited by Virginia Bianco-Mathis and Neal Chalofsky.
    p. cm.
  Includes bibliographical references and index.
  ISBN 0-7619-1222-3 (cloth: acid-free paper)
  ISBN 0-7619-1223-1 (pbk.: acid-free paper)
  1. Universities and colleges—United States—Faculty. 2. College teachers—United States—Social conditions. 3. College teaching—Vocational guidance—United States. 4. Education, Higher—United States. I. Bianco-Mathis, Virginia. II. Chalofsky, Neal, 1945-
  LB1778.2.F85 1998
  378.1'2'—ddc2   98-40062

This book is printed on acid-free paper.

99 00 01 02 03 10 9 8 7 6 5 4 3 2 1

Acquiring Editor:	Peter Labella
Editorial Assistant:	Renée Piernot
Production Editor:	Sherrise M. Roehr
Editorial Assistant:	Denise Santoyo
Typesetter/Designer:	Janelle LeMaster
Indexer:	Juniee Oneida
Cover Designer:	Candice Harman

Contents

Part II. Issues and Trends

Introduction

Academic Life and Career

Virginia Bianco-Mathis
Neal Chalofsky

It's a crisp, sunny day and Dr. Johnson is into the second month of the fall semester. He is a distinguished looking man—mid-40s, sandy blond hair that continually falls across his forehead, tweed jacket with elbow patches, occasional pipe. He has just spent 2 hours grading the first set of papers from his junior-year history class. During most of the morning, he held conferences with students. He is particularly excited about the research findings of one of his star doctoral students. It's now time for lunch, and he joins two of his colleagues walking down the paneled hallway. They walk through the large reception area—buzzing with students studying and sharing notes—and proceed to the private faculty dining room.

Lunch conversation is lively as several professors discuss the latest foreign policy agreement. Dr. Johnson starts a side conversation with Dr. Peters

AUTHORS' NOTE: Development of this book was made possible through a grant from the Consortium of Universities of the Washington Metropolitan Area, One Dupont Circle, NW, Suite 200, Washington, DC 20036-1166.

concerning a paper they will be presenting at a national conference. They both agree that more sources are needed in the reference section, and Dr. Johnson says he will get his research assistant to work on it right away.

After lunch, Dr. Johnson gathers his papers and books and walks to his class. Several students join him, and they proceed to the Wagner Building. The lecture goes well, and Dr. Johnson is pleased with the depth of questions. Several students follow him back to his office for more discussion.

Dr. Johnson then returns several telephone calls and makes it just in time to the department meeting. Most of the time is spent on curriculum changes because a documented rationale for all changes is due to the curriculum committee in 2 weeks.

At the end of the meeting, Dr. Johnson moves on to the library to conduct more research on a book he is writing. Noticing that it is getting late, he leaves, walks across campus, and enters the tree-lined neighborhood where many faculty live. He and his wife are due at the dean's house that evening to welcome a new department faculty member. He looks forward to a stimulating evening.

Present-day faculty read this account and wistfully smile. This kind of academic life no longer exists—if it ever did. A balanced workload, long philosophical discussions, adoring students hanging on your every word, and an enriching work environment now only exist in old movies and faculty fantasies. The academic world is dealing with the same outside influences as other businesses, government institutions, and industries: how to do more with less, rising costs, varying customer demands, multiple locations, technology, diversity, reengineering, quality improvement, outcomes assessment, and on and on. The pace and responsibilities of today's faculty member are quite expansive, and professors—whether junior or senior—need a road map to navigate their careers. If we lifted Dr. Johnson and transported him into today's world, he would be a bit shaken . . .

Dr. Johnson wakes up at 6:00 a.m., hops into her car, travels for 45 minutes along congested highways, gets to the main campus, finally finds a parking space several blocks from her office, and dashes to her first meeting. She is on the search committee for a new faculty member. It's going to be a long process because the committee received hundreds of resumes from around the world. The meeting runs for 2 hours. From here, Dr. Johnson jumps back into her car and drives across town to one of the university's six off-campus sites.

Most of the students in this particular business class have full-time jobs in the business world, and Dr. Johnson knows that the traditional lecture approach no longer works. She has spent several years converting all her material into interactive formats. The days of teaching the way she was taught are long gone. In fact, she recently had to fire an adjunct faculty member because he was not familiar or comfortable with alternative teaching approaches . . . which reminds her . . . she has to advertise for another adjunct faculty member. Because she is in charge of the new leadership certificate program, she is responsible for managing the courses and faculty for that portion of the curriculum.

The off-campus facility is quite spacious because it is provided by a national industry leader. A contract arrangement was made with the university to offer on-site business courses. Dr. Johnson enters the classroom, hooks herself up to the monitors at the front of the room, and waits for the technician to give her the OK sign. Suddenly, Dr. Johnson's image appears on six television monitors across the United States. She says hello to the 30 students in the room and the 500 satellite students and begins the lesson.

After class, it is time for a late lunch. Dr. Johnson grabs a sandwich at the corner deli, hops into her car, and heads to the main campus once again. On campus, she spends 2 hours counseling students through face-to-face meetings, and then spends another hour advising students over the telephone, through faxes, and via e-mail. She takes another hour to search for some new publications over the Internet. She prints out six articles and then decides to have dinner at the cafeteria. She sits down with several faculty members who are complaining about the new reorganization.

After dinner, Dr. Johnson goes to a nearby hotel, where she proceeds to give a guest presentation to one of the local professional societies. She likes this kind of event because she interacts with practitioners, shares her research, and also is able to market the new leadership certificate at the university.

As Dr. Johnson heads home, she begins to plan for the next day. She will be spending all day with her client, Acme Industries. She enjoys these occasional consulting assignments because they give her a chance to practice her theories—and, let's face it, they help pay the bills.

This kind of academic life requires a unique institutional infrastructure, and that's why universities and colleges are moving through much transition. Academic institutions are first trying to deal with new directions, including

- Main campus versus satellite locations
- Core curriculum versus contracts and certificate programs
- Teaching excellence versus research emphasis

They are also trying to manage diverse customer needs, encompassing

- A variety of populations, cultures, and expectations
- New technology requirements
- A wide range of programs
- A variety of formats and approaches

All these changes affect the decisions a faculty member must consider. That is why we developed this handbook. Choosing an academic career now involves a set of complicated factors that must be weighed and tested:

- Is my love teaching, research, or service?
- How does my personal agenda match that of the university or college I work at or want to work at?
- How do I manage my time?
- If I want to transfer to another university, how do the criteria or standards of my present college match those of others?
- Which committees must I sit on? Should I sit on?
- What research should I pursue?
- Which journals should I publish in?
- What outside endeavors am I expected to pursue? Not pursue?
- How do I work the system?
- Where or to whom do I go for advice?
- How do I get tenure?
- How do I get promoted?
- What are the written and unwritten rules?

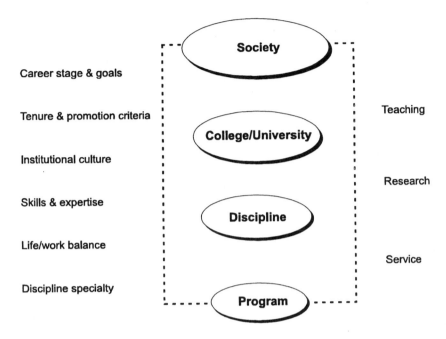

Figure I.1. The Professorial World

❖ THE PROFESSIONAL WORLD

Conceptually, we see the work of professors falling into four concentric circles or arenas (Figure I.1):

1. Program
2. Discipline
3. College/university
4. Society

Program

Your first "loyalty" is usually to the program area in which you teach. For most of us, no matter what type of college or university we are in, what we teach and the program we teach it in provide our primary identification. Although some faculty have joint appointments or multiple program responsibilities, most of us reside in one primary program. The other program faculty are usually our closest colleagues; we coordinate teaching schedules, attend meetings, discuss students, lament over the bureaucracy and our "unfair" salaries, and possibly work together on research and publishing efforts.

Discipline

You belong to an academic or professional discipline that provides the content of what you teach, speak, research, and write about. You probably belong to at least one, if not several, professional associations; and you have or will probably hold an office or serve on a committee in one of these organizations at the national or local level. One of your most important academic career goals, if not the most important, is to establish your reputation as a significant contributor to the knowledge and the advancement of your discipline (your "field"). Your tenure or contract renewal and promotions are dependent on your continued work in your discipline.

College or University

We are all employees of an institution that pays us a salary and benefits and provides us with some space and equipment to do our work. But more than that, the institution represents an environment that is unique to any other work organization. We hear a presentation from a notable person from our own or another discipline, watch a basketball game, work out or play racquetball at the gym, dine at the faculty club, review books at the library, and attend conferences all over the world. Being a faculty member at an institution of higher learning provides freedom, autonomy, and a variety of legitimate and sanctioned work activities unheard of in most other private or public organizations. What is also unheard of is the "collegial" form of governance most universities use. Such a governance body includes different entities (schools or colleges) within the university that not only decide faculty policy but influence academic and fiscal policies of the institution as well.

Society

Our hope is that all faculty also see they have a responsibility to their communities and the larger society, as well as the other three levels previously mentioned. We are expected to provide service to our communities and our professional associations. Beyond these basic requirement, we should be models to our students concerning the responsibilities we all have as "good citizens." We have expertise that we can share and we have time that the university accords us to be able to contribute to the common good.

❖ CAREER PATH

The depth and breadth of work across these areas will be influenced by personal preferences, expertise and interests, university expectations, and career developmental stage and goals. As a new professor, you will probably be guided by what will get you tenure or contract renewal. Once you have achieved some measure of stability, you will probably pursue activities that support building your reputation and lead to promotions. At some point, the path may shift to administration or into a primarily research mode. Lastly, you will reach a stage where you are ready to cut back or retire. Your path will be significantly influenced by what you find to be most meaningful and fulfilling.

This environment gives you a unique opportunity to pursue your passion and share it with others (students and colleagues). There are not too many jobs in our society where one is recognized and rewarded for doing research, teaching, advising, and conferencing in an area of study that one finds intellectually stimulating and challenging. Only the religiously or financially privileged could hope to be able to pursue such work in the past. What burns academics out is the university bureaucracy, not the work. Along with the freedom and autonomy come boring faculty and committee meetings; endless forms to fill out and procedures to follow; sometimes uncooperative and inflexible administrative staff to deal with; and clashes and conflicts with deans, department heads, colleagues, and students. How well you learn to "work the system" to avoid as much of the stress and frustration as possible that results from working in a bureaucracy will determine how comfortable your journey will be.

This book provides a sense of what being an academic is all about, as well as some ideas as to how to fulfill short- and long-term career goals successfully. The chapters sometime overlap because different authors discuss similar themes from their own point of view. A variety of styles is included in the book to capture the unique background of each author. Each contributor uses an honest approach with concrete examples and tips.

❖ PART I: ACADEMIC ROLES AND RESPONSIBILITIES

This part of the book lays out the work of a faculty member in an institution of higher learning. The first chapter in this section, "Administration and Management," by Nyla Carney and Teresa Long, covers the types of institutions of higher education, how you find out what a particular college or university is really like (its culture), and why it is important to learn all you can about the administrative and governance structure of your institution.

Chapter 2, "Teaching and Learning," by James J. Fletcher and Sondra K. Patrick, goes into a detailed discussion of the characteristics of exemplary teachers and learning styles. The authors review teaching methods and techniques and conclude with a section on learning objectives, syllabi development, grading, and self-assessment.

Chapter 3, "Student Advising," by Rosemarie Bosler and Sharon L. Levin, deals with both the academic and the personal issues surrounding advising and shares insights about advising students doing internships, theses, and dissertations.

Chapter 4, "Academic Research," by Sharon Ahern Fechter, covers why research is so important in higher education, how to establish a research agenda, how to tailor research to the university's and your own personal goals, and research in cyberspace.

The traditional third leg of the academic stool, service, is covered in the next two chapters (5 and 6). "University Service," by William J. A. Marshall, discusses the academic and political realities of serving on university committees and task forces. Marshall offers a lively discussion of managing your time and making meaningful choices. Chapter 6, "Professional Service," by Karen L. Medsker, discusses the advantages of participating in professional and academic associations, as well as attending local, national, and international conferences.

❖ PART II: ISSUES AND TRENDS

This part looks at current issues in academia and some of the changes taking place that will revolutionize the campus in the next millennium. In Chapter 7, "Professional Development and Advancement," Rhonda J. Malone talks about how to meld teaching, research, and service in such a way as to advance your career and develop yourself professionally. She discusses the tension between traditional and emerging viewpoints concerning tenure, status, contribution, and performance criteria.

Sharon Johnson Confessore, in Chapter 8, "New Learning Approaches," reconceptualizes the nature of learning in higher education based on changes that have already begun to affect academia.

Chapter 9, "Technology," by Theodore Stone, provides a view of how the Web and distance learning is already changing the way universities do business and how we need to take the notion of the virtual university seriously.

Chapter 10, "Diversity in Higher Education," by Mary Hatwood Futrell and Walter A. Brown, covers the responsibilities we all share to embrace the diversity of our student body and ourselves. It appropriately relabels the university the *multiversity*.

In the epilogue, we bring you back to our opening scenario of Dr. Johnson's daily routine and celebrate the excitement of being a faculty member in today's (and tomorrow's) institution of higher learning.

Part I

ACADEMIC ROLES
AND RESPONSIBILITIES

1

Administration and Management

Nyla Carney
Theresa Long

❖ UNDERSTAND THE ORGANIZATION'S CULTURE

Depending on your academic field, you may have several job offers pending even before your dissertation has been bound and processed. If this is the case, you are one of the fortunate ones. The truth is, however, that in many disciplines, finding a full-time tenure-track opening is not that easy. Necessity rather than choice may dictate your first doctorate-in-hand academic position. You should not regard taking a job because of necessity as a negative career move as long as you are prepared to make the most of the experience even if the position is not at the university of your dreams. The image of academics who retire from the college or university that first hired them is outdated. Even if you are lucky enough to have several enticing job offers to choose from, chances are you will change teaching institutions more than three times before retirement. In today's ever-volatile job market, you need to understand the goals, culture, and organizational structure of the various types of higher education institutions to make the most of your first full-time teaching job and to prepare for any future career transitions.

3

In the first part of this chapter, you will encounter a series of questions concerning your initial job search. These questions are designed to highlight the wide variety of institutions in higher education and to help you understand the teaching implications of their different organizational cultures. The questions in the second half of the chapter deal specifically with higher education administrative structure and management. The answers to these questions will give you more control over important aspects of your career such as promotion and tenure decisions. The purpose of this chapter is to emphasize the need to obtain specific information about the institution where you plan to teach to strengthen your membership in that academic community.

❖ TYPES OF INSTITUTIONS OF HIGHER EDUCATION

Although dissemination of knowledge is the heart and soul of all institutions of higher learning, the kinds of institutions that deliver this knowledge can be very different organizationally and culturally. The 1994 Carnegie classification of higher education (Carnegie Foundation, 1994) groups institutions into six broad categories:

- Research universities (types I and II)
- Doctoral universities (types I and II)
- Masters (comprehensive) universities and colleges (types I and II)
- Baccalaureate (liberal arts) colleges (types I and II)
- Associates of arts colleges
- Professional schools and specialized institutions

As you begin your job search, you should carefully consider the academic focus of the institutions in these six groups. Ideally, you want to apply to institutions whose educational goals and missions offer the best match with your own career objectives. Realistically, you need to be flexible.

The Carnegie classification includes 3,600 institutions of higher education. The six categories and their subgroupings categorize schools from two general perspectives: (1) the highest degree awarded—type I institutions award more degrees in the category than type II institutions, and (2) the academic focus of the institution, for example, research, professional, or occupational, liberal arts. This method of classification makes you realize the overall breadth and variety of institutions in the higher education system. This knowledge alone offers encouragement that somewhere among those 3,600 schools is a job with your name on the contract. Other important institutional factors, however, should figure in your decision of where to apply and what offer to accept.

❖ WHAT'S THE INSTITUTION REALLY LIKE?

Every institution has its own unique character that you will uncover only after teaching there. Yet you dramatically increase your chances of being called for an interview if you are well informed about the school ahead of time. Read all literature sent to you about the school.

Having served on faculty search committees, we know that if you demonstrate your compatibility with and knowledge of the university's educational mission, you will stand out in the minds of the search committee more than the candidate who sends the generic "I'm looking for a job" cover letter and application. The generic cover letter tells the committee that you are blanketing the market in search of whatever position is available and that any job will do. Although this may be the truth, your chances of making the final cut will be greatly enhanced if you show the committee that you have not only the required credentials but also the intelligence to market your talents wisely.

Sources of Information About the Institution

- Check the institution's Web site—get an overall sense of the campus.
- Read the catalog—know the structure of the curriculum.
- Look at student brochures—see how the institution portrays itself.

As you move closer to accepting a job offer, you will make a more informed career decision once you have checked out the above sources. By now you should have the answers to some basic questions:

1. What is the educational thrust of the school? Research institution—professional or occupational—liberal arts—other?
2. What is the total enrollment? Less than 2,000? More than 5,000? Over 10,000?
3. Is it public or private?
4. What does the general education curriculum look like?
5. What courses are offered in your teaching specialty? What are the requirements in the major?
6. Is your area of expertise compatible with the school's programs?

After answering these questions, if you cannot see yourself ever being happy teaching at that institution, keep looking. You need to decide how long you can afford to reject potential jobs because they do not quite fit into your career game plan, however. If this scenario repeats itself very often, you may need to reassess your short-term goals. On the other hand, if you are comfortable with the answers to your initial questions—or at least you have not ruled the position out entirely—you are ready to proceed to the next level of the search.

Points to remember:

- Never limit your search to any one type of institution.
- Keep your options open.
- Be willing to revise your short-term goals.
- Understand the culture of the institution.

❖ WHO ARE THE STUDENTS, AND
   WHAT IS EXPECTED OF THE FACULTY?

You should develop a fairly accurate profile of the student body. After all, the students you encounter daily in the classroom will most directly affect your job satisfaction. Next in importance to the students you teach are the expectations the institution has of its faculty. Be aware of the following facts concerning students and expected faculty duties before accepting any teaching position. These characteristics are crucial to identifying and understanding the culture of an institution and to ensuring that your first year will not hold a series of unpleasant surprises or disappointments. Ask questions and listen to the answers.

The student body:
1. Undergraduate or graduate focus
2. Commuters or residents
3. Academic preparedness
4. Degree of diversity

The faculty:
1. Teaching workload
2. Expected publications and research
3. Administrative duties
4. Type of governance structure

Student Profile

For institutions that offer baccalaureate and graduate degrees, what is the ratio of undergraduate to graduate students? Is the enrollment divided evenly between the two groups or not? As a new hire, will you have the opportunity to teach in all levels? If the school offers only one degree, will you be expected to cover a broad range of classes or will your teaching be more limited to specialized courses? The scope of your teaching opportunities may depend heavily on the composition of the student body.

A commuter versus a residential campus can add another dynamic to your choice of preferred school. If you see yourself as a mentor frequently meeting with students informally, you may be disappointed in a primarily commuter campus where many students maintain a rigorous schedule of work and school. At the same time, if you are teaching on a residential campus, you may do a lot of personal as well as academic counseling and consequently spend less time than you had planned on your own academic research.

Equally valuable in understanding the type of student you will encounter in class is an institution's admissions policy. How selective are the admissions criteria? What are the average SAT or ACT scores? Is the admissions policy open door? Do a large percentage of students enter with advanced placement credit from high school, or will some students in your class also be taking developmental courses in English or mathematics? Are you willing and ready to teach in both situations? How diverse is the student population? Is it racially and ethnically homogeneous? Are the students mostly traditional college age, or are they nontraditional returning adult students? Is there an international student presence on campus? Although these questions focus on gross stereotypes, having a clear picture in mind of the nature of an institution's student body is important. Each student element can play a positive, negative, or neutral role in your job decision process.

Faculty Expectations

What exactly does the school expect from you in addition to your classroom teaching? Does the teaching workload make it possible to achieve the level of scholarly research and publication that either you or the school wants? How much advising are you assigned? Is there a "service to the university" component in the rank and tenure policies? If so, how is service defined? Does the institution's governance structure require you to be an active participant—for example, are you required to serve on governance committees?

If you accept a position at this institution, can you teach your allotted number of classes, advise students, maintain your professional scholarship, participate in the school's organizational structure, and still manage to feed your dog at night? The answer will always be no. The point is, are you excited about attempting these impossible tasks at University X?

Once you have some understanding of the culture of an institution, weigh its pluses and minuses carefully. Understand how the institution's character will affect the position you are applying for and decide how satisfied you will be in that job. By this point in the search process, you should have a clear basis for your decision to refuse or accept an offer.

❖ ACCEPTING A LESS-THAN-PERFECT JOB

Perhaps you have been offered a position, but it is not at the type of institution you had envisioned nor will you be doing the type of teaching or research you set out to pursue. Job hunting in an overbooked discipline may force you to accept something less than "perfect." In fact, your first full-time position may be a temporary 1-year appointment!

Under these circumstances, stay marketable.

- Continue your scholarly and professional activities.
- Network with other faculty members in your discipline on and off campus.
- Learn your way around the academic system.
- Add new dimensions to your experience in both teaching and administration.

❖ THE STRUCTURE AND HOW IT WORKS

Accepting a teaching position does not always mean that your principle work involves being in the classroom or research lab. Actually, you will spend more time than you anticipate on administrative matters. For this reason, it is to your advantage to become very familiar with the exact structure of the institution you have just joined.

Although most colleges and universities are in reality very complex organizations, all are formally organized on very simple and similar lines (see Figure 1.1). Looking at the organization from the bottom up, you will most likely report to your department chair, who will report to the school or college dean, who will report to the vice president of academic affairs, who will report to the president, who will report to the board. Other functions of the university, such as enrollment management, financial affairs, institutional development, and student services, will have similar lines of organization. The layers of organizational structure depend on the size and diversity of the curriculum and student body. The vice presidents and above are generally classified as senior administration and are not usually part of the teaching faculty. Deans, associate or assistant deans, department chairs, and program directors are usually faculty positions that carry specific administrative responsibilities in lieu of some teaching or research responsibilities and may or may not rotate among the faculty.

Keep in mind your turn may come to serve as an administrative faculty, so it pays to learn something about the nature of these positions. Also keep in mind that many lines of communications and decision making follow informal structures; early on in your career, you should begin to watch for and identify these informal lines.

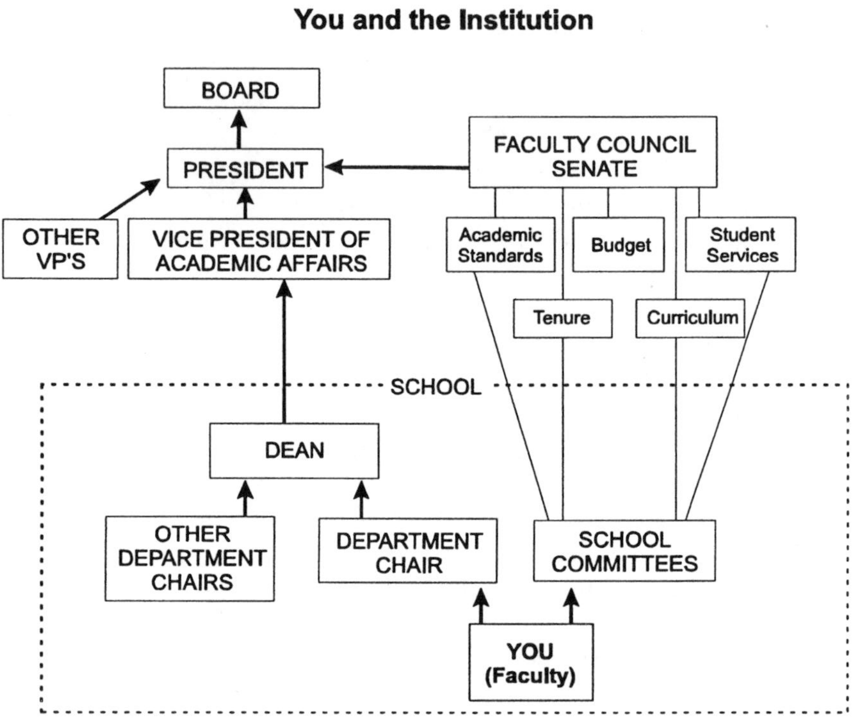

You and the Institution

Figure 1.1. Academic Structure

Looking at the organization from the top down, the board is primarily responsible for setting institutional policy (such things as the institution's mission and tenure decisions) and securing and allocating the necessary resources to fulfill that mission. The president's primary responsibilities are to carry out the directives and policies of the board by acting as the liaison among various units of the academic community and as the official representative of the institution to the public and its constituencies.

The primary responsibilities of vice presidents are to interpret and administer policies in their designated areas. For example, the vice president of academic affairs represents, interprets, and administers the academic programs through the academic budget, calendar, curriculum, faculty utilization, and planning; this is the individual from whom your dean or department chair receives directives.

Most important to you are the deans and department chairs. These are the individuals who have the greatest influence on your day-to-day activities and your professional development. They are also your primary link to upper-level decision making. These individuals determine your schedule (what you teach, when you teach, how you divide your energies among teaching, research, and service) and the available funding for your various activities. Officially, the dean interprets the directives of the vice president in both long-run planning and short-run operations of the school. This includes such things as budget control, faculty professional development and evaluation, student outcomes, and providing a link to the outside community. Department chairs are responsible for the day-to-day activities of the academic department, including the student advising system, curriculum development, teaching assignments, and assistance to the dean. Learn the answers to these questions:

1. To whom do you direct student problems, teaching requests, advising issues, grant applications?
2. How do you initiate curriculum changes?
3. Who will evaluate your annual performance, your promotion application, your tenure request?
4. How are advising assignments made?
5. How do you select or how are you elected or assigned to committee appointments?

It is in your best interest to observe and learn from the activities of your department chair or dean the formal and informal information and decision-making channels.

Looking at the organization from the inside, the faculty's role in the academic decision-making process generally emanates from the governance system that, through its committee structures, recommends policy and resources acquisition and utilization to a faculty council or senate, which then forwards the recommendations on to the president. Faculty governance systems are usually organized along the lines of faculty responsibilities. As identified in the *Policy Documents and Reports* (Kreiser, 1995) of the American Association of University Professors, faculty are generally responsible for the development and oversight of all academic areas that include curriculum, admission criteria, program completion standards, faculty hiring, performance evaluation, promotion, and tenure and student activities as related to these academic areas. These include such activities as advising, learning resources, and student athletics.

These responsibilities are usually fulfilled through a variety of forums and structures. Each academic department or school, as well as the college or university generally, has a committee structure to address issues of curriculum, faculty hiring, retention and performance evaluation, admission, academic performance criteria, and program completion requirements.

Recommendations for change may be initiated at any level—by an individual faculty member within a department, by a standing committee of the faculty governance council or senate, by the administration—but most progress through an identified procedure that includes faculty input at the department level, the school level, the standing committee level, and the faculty council or senate level. Often new faculty are elected or appointed to committees, because senior faculty are better able to resist committee work and because it is a way of testing new faculty members' philosophies and abilities to work in groups, and because it is part of the initiation into the promotion and tenure criteria of community service. So that you have some choice about your committee service, learn the answers to these questions:

1. Which committees do what and meet when?
2. Which committees are important and which are deadly?
3. Which committees are important to your agenda for the next several years?

Do not lose sight of the informal network, however. Effective committee service, meeting both the institution's needs and your needs, requires knowing how to work the system and how to build coalitions. This committee service also provides you as a new faculty member with contacts and liaisons to other colleagues throughout the university.

Aside from the fact that effective participation in the governance of the university is expected from a faculty member, your participation is important to your academic career. Although governance systems are often ineffective in the short run in directing the activities of the institution, active participation in this process influences the professional environment, including academic freedom, in which you pursue your career. Faculty governance systems reflect the administration's posture toward the inclusion of faculty input in the overall policy and operations of the university. This inclusion exerts influence on the academic quality and integrity of the institution and the resource allocation—both of which define the classroom environment in which you teach and conduct your research. It also exerts influence on the avenues for your professional development, retention, promotion, and tenure.

Despite all these laudatory statements about the importance of participating in the process, never expect any external reward or ongoing recognition for your efforts. This is the least acknowledged activity of faculty, and yet one of the most important in defining the tone of the your work life.

❖ ADMINISTRATIVE DUTIES

Expect the time and effort required in the administrative activities of faculty life to continue to grow. Higher education is experiencing a structural shift, maybe even an earthquake. The past, when most of the administrative and governance structures were designed, was characterized by continual and stable growth in student enrollment and, therefore, resources. In that environment, most university decision making involved how to allocate additional students and resources to existing programs or how to establish new programs. Those days are gone.

The challenge to academic decision making today and in the future is how to *reallocate* existing resources and how to redefine the educational mission, activities, and programs in the face of stable or declining enrollments and resources. This challenge involves not only the academic programs but also the other functional areas of the university—enrollment management, student services, external funding, and institutional development. Most existing administrative and governance structures are not designed to cross functional lines (or even departmental lines) and provide input to all areas of the university. Evidence of this lies in the growing number of ad hoc committees or strategic committees within the university and the growing emphasis by external agencies—state governments, regional accrediting agencies, and public interest groups—on demonstration of educational effectiveness. Faculty may expect an increased demand on their time and energies to assist their institution's attempts to meet this challenge.

Consequently, though you might have thought that you have to consider budgeting your time only when it comes to teaching, service, and scholarship, you must also consider a long list of administrative duties, even though becoming an administrator might not be one of your career goals. This means learning the management structure, politics, and general "how do you get things done around here" issues. These duties may include such diverse activities as serving on faculty search committees; working with adjunct faculty; managing certificate, internship, or other nondegree programs (including budgeting, staffing, and outcomes assessment); participating in self-studies of degree programs, academic majors, and the institution; and serving on ad hoc committees. In addition, there will be the random request from your dean or department chair to review and respond to inquiries from students, administration, higher education associations, advisory boards, and the like for information on new programs, budgetary items, community involvement, and so on and so on. . . .

Some of these duties are one-time activities—most likely your institution will not be engaged in an ongoing faculty search process. That also means that these activities are difficult to plan ahead for and incorporate into your semester schedule, however. Working with adjunct faculty may be very time-consuming at the beginning and end of the semester and require little time during the semester. Program or certificate coordination activities may be very time-consuming during certain times of the academic year (when budget requests or course schedules are due) and nonexistent at other times. Internal and external requests for analysis and recommendations often occur without much advanced warning and with short turnaround times. The lesson: Build some flexibility into your schedule for all these extra duties! Learn the answer to these questions (and plan accordingly):

1. What is happening to enrollment?
2. What ad hoc committees exist, why, and who serves on them?
3. What external agencies exert influence on the university, school, department?
4. What are the long-range plans of the university?
5. How has the organizational structure changed in the last 5 years?

6. What administrative duties should you expect to be involved in?
7. How would you like to participate?

Once you have compiled and assimilated the answers to the various questions contained in this chapter, you will have an accurate picture of an institution's organizational culture and administrative structure. You are now armed with the necessary information to become a productive member of that academic community. You have become empowered!

❖ REFERENCES

Carnegie Foundation for the Advancement of Teaching. (1994). *A classification of institutions of higher education.* (1994). Princeton, NJ: Author. (Eric Document Reproduction Service No. ED 374 754.)

Kreiser, R. B. (Ed.) (1995). *Policy documents and reports.* Washington, DC: American Association of University Professors.

❖ ADDITIONAL SOURCES

Birnbaum, R. (Ed.). (1991). *Faculty in governance: The role of senates and joint committees in academic decision making.* San Francisco: Jossey-Bass.

Roger, B., Carroll, S., Jacobi, M., Krop, C., & Shires, M. (1993). *The redesign of governance in higher education.* Santa Monica, CA: RAND.

2

Teaching and Learning

James J. Fletcher
Sondra K. Patrick

This book covers all aspects of the professional life of the full-time faculty member. Faculty responsibilities are usually described in terms of three roles: teaching, research, and service. Most institutions require that faculty make significant contributions in all these areas, but the emphasis differs from one institution to another. Hence, if you want to be successful in developing a long-term association with an institution, it is very important that you know the requirements for success at your institution. For faculty new to the profession, it is important to seek out a mentor who can advise you about the relative weight given to each of the professional roles in the local reward structure. Other chapters in this text provide general advice about academic research and university and professional service; this chapter addresses your role as a teacher. Although faculty typically go through several developmental stages during their professional lives, in which research, teaching, or service occupies a larger share of their time, teaching remains the center of academic life. Although our role as a teacher remains a constant, none of us can assume that one teaching strategy will work for all situations. Changing student populations and technologies are examples of two current forces that require us to rethink our approaches to instruction. One of the main goals of this chapter is to describe a wide range of teaching methods and techniques so that you can be flexible in addressing the variety of teaching challenges you will face.

There are no foolproof recipes for teaching because, as Kenneth Eble (1982) understands, teaching is fundamentally an interaction between the teacher and the learner. Each interaction is a unique experience, so the key to being a successful teacher is to approach a teaching situation with flexibility and to put students' needs to understand ahead of your need to profess. Although teaching is very individualized, recent research indicates that exemplary teachers share some characteristics. We also can derive some generalizations from the available research about learning.

In this chapter, we begin with an overview of the characteristics of exemplary teachers and a discussion of learning styles. We then review teaching methods and techniques from which faculty may choose, explaining the features of each, the circumstances under which each may be used most beneficially, and some of the widely used variations of these techniques. We conclude the chapter by applying the discussions of learning styles and teaching methods to the development of a course. This concluding section begins with a discussion of learning objectives and explains how to establish objectives for the course and for individual lessons. Suggestions for developing a syllabus are then provided, followed by sections on grading student work and techniques for assessing your own performance. Throughout the chapter, we provide checklists, tables, examples, and appendixes that offer concrete suggestions for developing syllabi, lesson plans, and assessment strategies that can be easily applied to classroom situations.

❖ EXEMPLARY TEACHING

Research based on student and faculty views about characteristics of good teaching reveals a high degree of agreement on a number of features (Centra, 1993; Cohen, 1981; Feldman, 1976, 1988). Among the characteristics most often cited by students and faculty alike are knowledge, clarity, organization and preparation, enthusiasm, and stimulation (Sherman et al., 1987). The first three refer primarily to the content of the teaching experience; the last two relate closely to the faculty member's ability to engage students in the learning experience. A little reflection reveals why these characteristics are central to good teaching. Let us begin with knowledge.

It should be obvious that a good teacher has to have mastery of the subject matter of a course, but exemplary teachers are those who have "a passion for the subjects they teach and a sincere desire to pass this knowledge on to their students" (Sherman et al., 1987, p. 70). An excellent teacher also understands the interrelationships between the subject under discussion and other fields of knowledge and is able to articulate those connections to students.

Articulating connections is also an important aspect of the characteristic referred to as *clarity*. You may know everything there is to know about your subject, but you will not succeed as a teacher if you are unable to communicate this knowledge clearly to your students. Clarity involves skill in speaking to groups large and small, but more is involved than public speaking skills. It requires the ability to simplify and articulate complex concepts and to be sensitive about whether students have understood your explanation (Sherman et al., 1987, p. 68). One way of putting this is to say that successful teachers approach their subjects from the point of view of their students. They develop lesson plans that start from the perspective of a novice and then build toward complexity. Students assimilate new knowledge in terms of structures and content they already know (McKeachie, 1994), so clarity requires that the teacher be sensitive to the level of the course and the extent to which students might have familiarity with the content under consideration. If the material is likely to be completely unfamiliar, it is important to use examples, anecdotes, and metaphors that draw on students' experiences.

Organization and preparation refer to the manner in which a teacher structures the course or individual lesson. After knowledge of the subject matter, organization is the most critical element of good teaching because a well-organized lesson or course enables the student to understand where a faculty member is going with a point and how the parts of the lesson or course fit together. Organization also provides a structure by which the faculty member can develop more and more complex connections. In this regard, it is very important to develop course and lesson objectives. We discuss objectives in more detail in the third part of this chapter. For our present purposes, it is sufficient to note that by developing objectives, you are determining what you want to achieve for yourself as an instructor and for your students as learners. In a preliminary way, we can think of objectives as a set of questions that we pose about the course and its content. These questions become the points around which we organize the course or lesson. If your course or lesson is well organized, you should be able to develop an outline that shows the progression of the points you intend to make. It is a good idea to create outlines for lessons and to share them with students so that they can more readily follow presentations.

Preparation refers to the indispensable time you spend outside of class researching and thinking about how to present the material so that you can successfully achieve your objective(s). As Sherman et al. (1987) point out, however, preparation and organization do not mean rigidity. A well-organized and well-prepared professor should anticipate that student needs and interests may draw the lesson in unexpected directions. An exemplary teacher is flexible enough to accommodate new ideas within the structure of the lesson. The lesson and course organization should reflect the fact that learning involves cognitive and affective growth and development. Successful learning experiences are those that are organized around projects and assignments that model and reinforce the goal(s) established by the instructor.

Through the work of researchers like Benjamin Bloom (1956), we have a better understanding of the way learners process the information they receive. Bloom developed a taxonomy[1] (see Table 2.1) of the cognitive domain to simplify our understanding of the learning process that, according to his analysis, necessarily progresses from the concrete to the abstract. Each higher level of cognitive operation depends on the preceding level. The top of Table 2.1 corresponds to the most concrete levels, the bottom corresponds to the most abstract. The table provides a classifying name, description of the level of operation, and some examples of typical learning activities associated with each level. The importance of Bloom's taxonomy for our purposes is that it helps us think about the appropriateness of the objectives that we set for our courses and the importance of associating assignments with the objectives.

Frequently, faculty think that they are providing students with learning experiences that cover the full range of the cognitive domain. They are disappointed when they receive responses from their students that are, for example, merely descriptive, lacking in any real synthesis or

Table 2.1 Application of Bloom's Taxonomy to Teaching and Learning

Cognitive	*Definition*	*Illustrative Behavior*	*Teaching Method/ Assignment*
Knowledge of specifics	Recall of isolable bits of information, e.g., terms, facts, conventions, trends, categories, criteria, theories, and principles	Define, Identify, List, Name	Lecture/Multiple choice, Short answer
Comprehension of literal and symbolic messages	Translation, interpretation, and extrapolation	Explain, Retell in one's own words, Describe, Predict, Compare	Lecture, Questioning/ Short answer, Essay, Book review, Lab analysis
Application	Verifying theoretical knowledge through simple solving	Formulation, Use, Calculate, Apply, Derive	Lecture, Discussion, Demonstrate, Case study/Experiments, Role-playing
Analysis of material into its constituent parts	Identifying or classifying elements, relationships, or organizational principles	Analyze, Identify, Contrast, Solve	Cooperative learning, Groups/Seminars, Papers
Synthesis	Processing or combining elements into new patterns or organizations	Develop, Plan, Design, Write, Perform, Produce	Seminars/Independent study, Group projects, Peer teaching
Evaluation	Making judgments of the value of an idea, work, solution, etc., by the application of specific criteria and standards	Judge, Assess, Evaluate	Portfolios, Journals, Critical essays

evaluation. Upon closer examination of the actual assignments and teaching strategies that the instructor used, however, one often finds that the entire learning experience was presented at the lower end of Bloom's (1956) taxonomy. If we want students to engage in higher-order thinking, such as synthesis and evaluation, we must arrange learning experiences to ensure that this happens.

Thus, we cannot expect students to acquire a facility for analysis and evaluation if they spend their time listening to lectures. Lectures are suitable for presenting facts, but they do not provide students with an opportunity to engage the material in more active ways. Similarly, multiple choice tests are useful for determining how well students have mastered the facts of a lesson or course section, but they do not give students an opportunity to engage in analysis and synthesis. We must provide models for students of the cognitive behavior appropriate for our disciplines.

A further point about levels of cognitive experience concerns course levels. When we introduce students to new material in introductory courses, we should be sensitive to the fact that students process information in terms of knowledge they already possess. With a new subject area, we have to spend time orienting students by providing the basic terms, facts, events, and so on appropriate for the discipline. As the course progresses, we should build on that knowledge by requiring more complex and abstract exercises of cognitive behavior. Also, in upper-level and graduate courses, we must assess the level of knowledge students bring to our courses as a basis for the objectives that we set. We discuss course and assignment objectives in more detail in the third part of this chapter.

In addition to their concern for what is taught, exemplary teachers spend considerable time determining the most effective means of presenting the subject matter. This brings us to enthusiasm and stimulation. The *craft* of teaching to which Eble (1982) refers, when well practiced, keeps students positively engaged with the subject matter; enthusiasm and stimulation are central to student engagement. Learning occurs most effectively when students become emotionally involved in what they are studying. As Epstein (1981) points out, teaching is a performing art, so teachers must have a good command of communication skills suitable for dealing with small and large groups and with individuals on a one-to-one basis. Interestingly, enthusiasm seems to be the most widely cited characteristic of excellent teachers (Bridges, Ware, Brown, & Greenwood, 1971). Enthusiasm refers first to the faculty member's presence in the classroom. That is, an enthusiastic faculty member operates at a high energy level no matter what the time of the class and has a lively and varied delivery. Perhaps more important, however, is that the enthusiastic faculty member has a love for the subject and for teaching that is readily apparent to the students and that students describe as "contagious" or "infectious" (Sherman et al., 1987, p. 68).

The fifth characteristic of exemplary teachers is their ability to stimulate their students to become interested in the subject matter. Students will not be motivated to become involved in the learning experience if their intellectual curiosity has not been awakened. In many courses, faculty members find that students already are interested in the subject matter, but this is not always the case, especially if you are teaching a required support course for a related discipline. Exemplary teachers find ways to engage their students actively in the course material and help them see the significance and relevance of the course material from multiple perspectives. The choice of teaching strategies has a lot to do with maintaining student interest; we discuss these in detail in the next section of the chapter.

In addition to the five characteristics just discussed, a faculty member's personal qualities and demeanor play an important role in the teaching experience. Successful teaching experiences are highly dependent on the existence of rapport between the teacher and students. Establishing rapport requires that students be comfortable with the learning environment. Of course, the learning experience is equally dependent on the personal characteristics that students bring. As Joseph Lowman (1995) notes,

> In reality, a classroom is a highly emotional interpersonal arena in which a wide range of psychological phenomena occur. For example, students' motivation to work will be reduced if they feel that they are disliked by their instructor or controlled in heavy-handed or autocratic ways. All students are vulnerable to such disrupting emotions, and some students are especially sensitive to them. (p. 26)

It seems obvious that learning is more likely to occur in an environment of trust and that students will respond positively to a faculty member who comes across as caring, approachable, and respectful. Most students respond more readily to faculty whom they believe are concerned with their welfare, open to considering other points of view, respectful of students, available to discuss matters relating to the course, and willing to deal fairly with them.

Motivating students to do their best work can be one of the most challenging aspects of teaching. As James Davis (1993) notes, student motivation is complex, and no single strategy or device will work with all students. Still, an instructor can do much to maintain the interest that students bring to a course. In Figure 2.1, adapted from Barbara Davis

(1993, pp. 194-201), we outline some strategies that, if practiced, will help develop student motivation.

Just as faculty exhibit definite preferences for certain instructional methods, students have definite preferences for how they learn. One of the most important things faculty can do to enhance learning is to use a variety of teaching methods. In so doing, faculty increase the likelihood that their styles of presentation will match students' styles of learning.

❖ LEARNING STYLES

Attention to learning styles is relatively recent in educational studies. Theorists differ in their explanations of the preferences that students exhibit (J. Davis, 1993). Some attribute them to physiological factors (Sagan, 1977), others to personality types (Holland, 1966; Kolb, 1984; Myers & McCaulley, 1985), and still others to differences in sensing modalities (Barbe & Swassing, 1979). Whatever the causes of the differences, all theorists refer to "individuals' characteristic and preferred ways of gathering, interpreting, organizing, and thinking about information" (B. Davis, 1993, p. 185).

It would be unrealistic to expect faculty members not in the field of educational psychology to be aware of the various versions of learning theories and their implications for classroom practice. One study postulates at least 16 models of learning styles (Claxton & Murrell, 1987); adding multiple cognitive dimensions to these models complicates the matter even further (Grasha, 1984; Messick & Associates, 1976). For the faculty member in the classroom trying to be an effective instructor, the important thing is to remain aware that, whatever the reason, students process information in a variety of ways and, therefore, the more variety you use, the more likely a student's particular preference will be addressed.

Some students prefer to work independently, whereas others work well in groups. Some students approach problem solving in a linear, analytic fashion, whereas others prefer a holistic approach. Some students learn more easily with auditory input and, hence, prefer situations in which they are talking and listening. Students with auditory preferences are more comfortable in a learning environment that uses lectures and class discussions. Students who are more visually oriented prefer

General Strategies
- Capitalize on students' existing needs.
- Make students active participants in learning.
- Ask students to analyze what makes their classes motivating.

Instructional Behaviors That Motivate Students
- Hold high but realistic expectations.
- Help students set achievable goals.
- Tell students what they must do to succeed in your course.
- Avoid creating intense competition among students.
- Be enthusiastic about what you teach.

Structuring the Course to Motivate Students
- Work from students' strengths and interests.
- Let students have some say in what will be studied.
- Increase the difficulty of the material as the semester progresses.
- Vary your teaching methods.

De-emphasize Grades
- Emphasize mastery and learning rather than grades.
- Design tests that encourage the kind of learning you want students to achieve.
- Avoid using grades as threats.

Respond to Student Work
- Give students feedback as quickly as possible.
- Reward success.
- Introduce students to the good work done by their peers.
- Be specific when giving negative feedback.
- Avoid demeaning comments.

Get Students to Do the Reading
- Assign the reading at least two sessions before it will be discussed.
- Assign study questions.
- Ask students to write a 1-page journal or a 1-word sentence.
- Start with general questions about the reading.
- Prepare an exam question on undiscussed reading.
- Give written assignments to students who have not done the reading.

Figure 2.1. Motivating Students
SOURCE: B. Davis (1993), pp. 194-201.

situations in which they are reading or writing the information they need to learn. For such students, the act of note taking is an integral part of learning during a lecture or discussion. Visually oriented students might even prefer to work on projects or to keep a journal as a means of learning a subject area.

In the classroom setting, it is not likely that an instructor will know the learning style preference of each student. In fact, students may not even be aware of their own preferences. An instructor can provide a useful service by getting students to think about how they process new information. Simply asking students to take note of how they approach a problem and what actions they perform in learning new material will provide a clue as to the type of learning style they prefer. Surveys and checklists are available for faculty who wish to undertake a more systematic analysis of their students' learning styles. A good review of techniques for helping students to recognize their learning styles is provided by Barbara Davis (1993) in *Tools for Teaching*.

Most faculty, especially those teaching large classes, will not have the opportunity to discover the learning style of each student. Still, recognizing that students approach learning in diverse ways can be useful when trying to understand the differences in students' grasp of the material being presented. Variety in the way the material is presented and in the tools used to assess student performance will improve the learning experience for students and make the teaching experience more enjoyable for you because you will be a more effective teacher. In the next section of this chapter, we review a variety of teaching methods and techniques available, discuss their strengths and weaknesses, and provide hints for making effective use of them.

❖ TEACHING METHODS AND TECHNIQUES

Understanding the wide array of teaching methods and tools available to faculty today can help you determine the best approach for achieving course and lesson objectives. Pregent (1994, p. 75) asserts that there is no one "best" teaching strategy and that the decision about which to use depends to a large extent on the following five factors:

- the nature of the students in the class;
- the subject matter;
- the professor's personality;
- the physical and material conditions; and
- the targeted objectives.

Pregent (1994) also claims that student-centered teaching methods are "more conducive to significant learning, and more likely to increase memorization and learning transfer than 'professor-centered' methods" (p. 78). Instructional strategies that engage students in the learning process stimulate critical thinking and a greater awareness of other perspectives (Halpern, 1996). In effect, if we want students to be more involved and engaged in the learning experience, then they should be required to undertake activities related to the content, such as responding to questions posed by the instructor, writing a brief summary of key points, or engaging in whole group or small group discussions. We believe that all learning environments and all teaching methods can incorporate techniques that actively involve students. In this section, we discuss three basic teaching methods—lecture, discussion, and using groups. We also cover an assortment of teaching techniques that can be used in combination with any of the methods to cover the content of a lesson while actively engaging students.

The term *active learning* is heard frequently on college campuses today and is defined in a variety of ways. We prefer the description given by Meyers and Jones (1993) in *Promoting Active Learning: Strategies for the College Classroom*. They say that active learning occurs when students are allowed to *"talk and listen, read, write,* and *reflect* as they approach course content through problem-solving exercises, informal small groups, simulations, case studies, role-playing, and other activities—all of which require students to *apply* what they are learning" (p. xi). Active learning involves such strategies as:

- Requiring students to read, discuss, write, and/or question during the learning experience, not merely listen
- Encouraging higher-order thinking (application, analysis, synthesis, evaluation) by asking students to brainstorm possible solutions to a current problem or to write a 1-page idea paper about how they might apply a lesson concept to a current problem
- Providing time for student reflection about what they learned from a lesson by asking them to write or discuss the strengths and weaknesses of a particular concept or to identify one or more possible solutions or alternatives

The role of the instructor is different in a student-centered, active learning environment than in a more traditional, teacher-centered environment. Some faculty have expressed concern about using active learning techniques because they will not be able to cover as much material and because the success of the learning experience is so closely tied to students' attendance patterns and willingness to prepare and participate. Although instructors using active learning techniques tend to cover less material than instructors presenting a traditional lecture, the trade-off is worth it because students learn more (B. Davis, 1993; Halpern, 1996).

Another factor that inhibits faculty from trying active learning techniques is class size. Many faculty are required to teach large sections, and they find it especially difficult to keep large groups of students engaged. Later in this chapter, we provide some tips that can help address this problem. But first, let's examine the three basic teaching methods.

Lecture Method

The lecture method is the most widely used instructional strategy in college classrooms, and there are many occasions when it is the most appropriate means of disseminating information. Given what we know about students' attention, however, faculty should be careful about its use. As reported by McKeachie (1994), the research by Hartley and Davies (1978) demonstrates that a student's attention begins to decrease after 10 minutes. At the end of a lecture, students are able to recall 70% of what they heard during the first 10 minutes but only 20% of what was said in the last 10 minutes. If a lecture is to be effective, students must be attentive throughout. Incorporating active learning techniques into the traditional lecture will result in a more effective learning experience.

Because we know that it is often hard for students to remain attentive throughout a lecture session, we provide the following suggestions to help you keep your students mentally engaged:

- Assign each student a key topic to research and report on when the issue is discussed in class.
- Ask students to write for 1 minute about something they learned during the class session or about an issue or concept they do not understand.
- Encourage students to reflect on a particular content-related point, then lead a 5-minute discussion about alternative ways to address it.

- Design your course so that each student or each small group of students has the opportunity at least once during the course to make a 5-minute presentation on a key word or concept that will be discussed during a session. For this strategy to be successful, students need to be given this assignment 2 or 3 weeks in advance.

Lectures do not stand by themselves in a course. Treat the course as a series of learning segments so that you can insert an appropriate teaching technique to reinforce key concepts or pose questions that help students think about issues from multiple perspectives. In addition to these suggestions, using case studies or role-playing activities can be effective ways to involve students. Both techniques are discussed later in the chapter. As you think about the lecture you are to deliver, divide the task into three parts: preparation, presentation, and assessment. Appendix 2.1 outlines some important considerations under each part.

Discussion Method

Like lectures, discussions require a great deal of preparation, planning, and monitoring to be successful. For example, you decide the principal points to be covered, the preferred order for covering these points, and the session format; thus, you maintain a great deal of control over the learning experience. On the other hand, discussions differ significantly from lectures in the degree of student participation. Acting as a facilitator and guide, you monitor the discussion, encourage students to express their points of view, and assist students in supporting their opinions with arguments and references to texts or other relevant materials. For a discussion to be successful, students must come to class and be prepared to participate.

There are many ways to stimulate discussion. Sometimes it is useful to begin a lesson with a whole group discussion to refresh students' memories about the assigned reading(s). Other times it is helpful to have students provide a list of key points or generate a set of questions stemming from the assigned reading(s). These strategies can be used to focus large or small group discussions. You must exercise patience, however, allowing time for students to think about the topic and form responses. One rule of thumb, after posing a question, is to count to 10 before speaking again. Too often, faculty do not allow enough silence between asking a question and waiting for a student response. Below are some suggestions for using the discussion method effectively:

- Center the discussion around the lesson's topic.
- Help students prepare for a discussion during class by posing a question and then giving students time to write down ideas before responding.
- Ask students to write two questions they have about the assigned reading before coming to class.
- Consider providing students with a series of study questions several class sessions before a topic or issue is covered.
- When appropriate, ask students to describe how the discussion topic relates to their own experiences.

When using the discussion method, instructors worry about how to get students involved and still achieve course objectives. You should communicate to students an expectation that they attend regularly, complete assignments on time, and participate in the discussions. McKeachie (1994) reminds us that there are many reasons why students fail to participate in class discussions such as "boredom, lack of knowledge, general habits of passivity—but most compelling is a fear of being embarrassed" (p. 42). Getting students to talk to each other during the first weeks of class can be an important initial strategy for involving them in subsequent discussions as the course progresses (B. Davis, 1993; McKeachie, 1994). If your institution's facilities support it, we recommend that you use electronic communication to stimulate thinking about discussion topics between class meetings. Following are suggestions for managing discussions effectively:

- Don't be afraid of silence; give students time to reflect on the question you pose.
- Keep the discussion focused by listing points as they are made and relating them specifically to the topic.
- Use body language and facial expressions to encourage participation.
- Allow disagreement, but avoid heated exchanges.
- Be prepared with a new task or issue when the discussion runs its course.

Group Method

Much has been written about the importance of helping students learn to work together to prepare them better for both work and social roles. Increasingly, more faculty are trying to create interactive learning experiences that give students opportunities to work together to examine complex issues from multiple perspectives. It is not sufficient, however, simply to put students into groups and expect them to work well together. In fact, the effective use of groups requires careful planning, monitoring, and assessing.

The two most widely discussed strategies for using the group method are cooperative learning and collaborative learning. *Cooperative learning* is a systematic, active, pedagogical strategy that encourages small groups of students to work together for the achievement of a common goal (Johnson, Johnson, & Holubec, 1993). The five basic elements that separate it from other forms of group strategies are carefully articulated . by Johnson, Johnson, and Smith (1991, p. 3:16). Their definitions are provided below:

- Positive interdependence: Students need each other to complete a cooperative learning activity. This need is reinforced by establishing mutual goals, joint rewards, shared resources, and assigned roles.
- Face-to-face promotive interaction: Students support each other by sharing what they know and explaining what others do not understand.
- Individual accountability: Students are responsible for the group's successful completion of a cooperative learning activity. Frequently, an individual's grade is closely linked to the group's grade, or group members are asked to grade each others' performance and contribution.
- Interpersonal and small group skills: Students need to develop interpersonal, leadership, and decision-making skills.
- Group processing: Students need reflective time to assess their group's progress and discuss issues of concern or resolve any conflicts that may have developed.

Compared with more traditional, individualistic teaching methods, cooperative learning promotes higher-order thinking skills such as application, analysis, synthesis, and evaluation (Gabbert, Johnson, &

Johnson, 1986; Skon, Johnson, & Johnson, 1981). Cooperative learning strategies were initially developed for use in K-12 teaching environments. In such environments, students are in contact with one another for extended periods on a daily, or almost daily, basis. These extended periods of interaction provide the opportunity for the teacher to ensure that the five features described are implemented. In most higher education learning environments, conditions for extended interaction rarely exist except in programs where learning communities are specifically designed for regular and prolonged working relationships among students.

In higher education, the term *collaborative learning* is often mistakenly used as a synonym for cooperative learning when, in fact, it is a separate strategy that encompasses a broader range of group interactions (Cuseo, 1992; Smith & MacGregor, 1992) such as developing learning communities, stimulating student-faculty discussions, and encouraging electronic exchanges (Bruffee, 1993). In collaborative learning, one can expect to find one or more, but not necessarily all, of the five characteristics described above. Both approaches, however, stress the importance of faculty and student involvement in the learning process.

When integrating cooperative or collaborative learning strategies into a course, you must carefully plan and prepare. Your role is that of a facilitator and guide. Understanding various strategies for forming groups (Johnson et al., 1993; Johnson et al., 1991; Millis & Cottell, 1998), resolving group conflict (Johnson & Johnson, 1995), developing appropriate assignments and grading criteria, and effectively managing active learning environments are critical to the achievement of a successful group learning experience (Johnson et al., 1991). Table 2.2 outlines tips and strategies for successfully using the group method. A useful discussion on selected cooperative learning structures can be found in "Connecting with Cooperative Learning" by Barbara Millis (1996). Appendix 2.2 provides examples of different collaborative learning situations.

Teaching Techniques

Case Studies

Providing an opportunity for students to apply what they learn in the classroom to real-life experiences has proven to be an effective way of both disseminating and integrating knowledge. The case method is

Table 2.2 Using Groups: Tips and Strategies

Group Issues	Features	Strategy
Establishing groups	Size	Most effective groups have 4 to 6 members
	Assigning members	Homogeneous use gender, major, topic interest Heterogeneous use birth month, last digit of telephone number, counting off by group size
Group process	Faculty tasks	Establish roles within group (e.g., facilitator, reporter, and recorder) Be explicit and clear about group assignments Be explicit that all members must participate
	Expected student behavior	Prepare all assignments Attend regularly and on time Share ideas within group Be a good listener Respect others' opinions Don't dominate discussion
	Conflict	Some conflict is desirable, allow students to disagree and argue about ideas, urge reaching consensus Some conflict is destructive if based on lack of respect, domination, or failure to contribute Try to get the group to resolve the conflict themselves before intervening In extreme cases the offending member may have to be removed
Evaluation	Grading	Criteria must be clear and directly related to assignment Will students receive individual or group grade? Allow students to assess their own performance and that of the group members
Faculty role	Explain Establish Monitor Facilitate Encourage	Importance of group work to course Ground rules for participation Group progress Guide, explain, suggest strategies Performance and conflict resolution

an instructional strategy that engages students in active discussion about and investigation of real-world issues and problems. This technique can highlight fundamental social dilemmas or current issues in professional fields and can provide a format for role-playing ambiguous or contro-versial scenarios. We offer the following suggestions for successfully using case studies:

- Select cases that are appropriate for a course.
- Select cases that are engaging and encourage discussion.
- Prepare students for case study learning by demonstrating how to read and apply a case study; it might be helpful to prepare a set of guidelines or questions that will help students prepare a case.
- Consult with colleagues who have used case studies in their teaching to gain a better understanding of what works and what does not work effectively.

Although whole group discussion is the most widely used case study format developed by the Harvard Business School, Millis (1994) suggests that cooperative learning techniques can also be effective in presenting case studies. Forming small groups and allowing each group to examine a different case and report to the class is one effective way of using several related cases simultaneously to raise a variety of critical issues.

The role-playing technique can also be used with case studies. It provides a way for groups or individual students to demonstrate the issues addressed in particular cases actively and dramatically.

Cases for use in a course come from a variety of sources. Many faculty have transformed current events or problems reported through print or broadcast media into critical learning experiences that illuminate the complexity of finding solutions to current social problems such as HIV, homelessness, and environmental pollution. The case study approach works well in cooperative learning or role-playing environments to stimulate critical thinking and an awareness of other perspectives. It can also be effective when used to supplement a lecture, giving students an opportunity to apply lecture points to a real-life situation immediately.

Role-Playing

Role-playing generally involves a small group of students who are asked to dramatize a real-world or hypothetical situation or experience (B. Davis, 1993). For example, the assignment may be to make a situation come to life by putting oneself in the shoes of another, using imagination to re-create a scene in a novel, reenacting a historically important moment in time, or illuminating a particular social dilemma or controversial political issue. We suggest the following considerations for successfully using role-playing experiences with students (McKeachie, 1994):

- Allow students to volunteer for role-playing experiences.
- Impose time limits for each role-playing activity.
- Allow two or three groups to perform the same role-playing experience to demonstrate multiple perspectives.
- Allow students who participate in a role-playing activity to discuss their interpretation after the performance and before class discussion.
- Provide guidelines for students who are observing the role-playing experience.

As with all teaching techniques, role-playing activities work best when used to support learning objectives. When used sparingly, they tend to generate interest and rich discussion. If overused, they tend to become routine and unexciting (McKeachie, 1994; Meyers & Jones, 1993).

Peer Teaching

Peer teaching occurs when students are given the opportunity to teach other students in a learning experience. Students can be a valuable resource of knowledge, experience, and expertise. In addition, they learn at different paces and apply what they have learned in different ways that are often new and exciting. Faculty should use this valuable resource to their advantage. Activities that center around a course project or a problem-based learning assignment can be useful occasions for helping students recognize their strengths and teaching them how to share them with others. The peer teaching technique works well with both the discussion method and the group method, where students are given opportunities to share their ideas with an entire class or with a small group of students. Education today is a cooperative endeavor, and not everything that is learned has to come from the teacher. As with most active learning techniques, the role of the instructor is that of guide and facilitator.

Questioning

Questioning is an important technique for involving students in the learning experience. Questions can be used with any of the three basic teaching methods. For example, providing students with a list of study questions before a lecture can help guide them through difficult material and help them raise content-related questions of their own. Unfortunately, students frequently come to us with underdeveloped thinking and questioning skills. They have been taught to receive knowledge rather than create it. Using questions to help students find creative and innovative solutions to complex problems can help them develop higher-order thinking skills (Halpern, 1996).

Be aware that posing different kinds of questions can be an effective way of moving students through the levels of a complex concept you want them to understand. Barbara Davis (1993, p. 84) identifies 10 kinds of questions: exploratory questions, challenge questions, relational questions, diagnostic questions, action questions, cause-and-effect questions, extension questions, hypothetical questions, priority questions, and summary questions. Some questions merely ask students to recall information, but others move students to new levels of cognitive development by asking them to think about causal connections or to consider new applications, new associations, or new evaluating criteria. Depending on the point you want to make, be sensitive to the kind of questions you are posing. Table 2.3 correlates samples of different types of questions with desirable learning objectives.

Course Environments

Today, learning environments can take many shapes and forms. Although some may be more traditional in appearance (a room with chairs arranged in rows and instructor's desk in the front), technology is making it possible for academic learning experiences to occur any place a group of people gathers to exchange ideas and learn from each other. Here we discuss three kinds of learning environments that often influence the types of teaching methods an instructor can use.

Lab Sections

Laboratory environments are ideal settings for teaching applications. Johnson and Johnson (1995) assert that laboratory instruction

Table 2.3 Questions, Learning Objectives, and Cognitive Behaviors

Type of Question	Learning Objective	Cognitive Behavior
Factual *What is the definition of . . . ?*	Background knowledge, basic understanding of material	Recall, Define
Comparative *How is a ballad different from free verse?*	Relating ideas, issues, theories, or individuals	Compare, Differentiate
Cause-effect *What is the effect of fluorocarbons on the ozone layer?*	Asks for causal relationships, connects seemingly unrelated material or concepts	Connect, Interpret, Develop, Analyze, Hypothesize
Action *How should the Fed respond to increased wage pressures?*	Requires a conclusion or action	Analyze, Apply, Solve, Prioritize
Critical *What about _____ as an alternative explanation?*	Requires a challenge to the premises or argument under	Critique, Judge, Challenge, Justify
Evaluative *Which explanation of the Civil War is better?*	Requires an assessment of the relative value of the items under consideration	Evaluate, Judge, Assess
Extension *How does the* Declaration of Independence *build on Locke's political philosophy?*	Relates the discussion to material already covered	Synthesize, Expand, Create

takes students away from the theoretical setting of the textbook and lecture, to confront them with problems to solve, experiments to conduct, demonstrations to observe, exercises to complete, short-term and long-term projects to pursue, or data to collect so they can interpret and draw conclusions. (pp. 90-91)

Although laboratory settings can be effective learning spaces, they present special problems for instruction. The most common problems are higher noise levels and more distractions for students. For example, in computer labs, students often want to use computers for checking personal e-mail and exploring Internet Web sites. When these activities occur during times when instructors are giving lesson assignments and directions, the clicking of the keyboard can be very distracting. To minimize these distractions, you need to establish lab use guidelines, carefully plan each lesson and assignment, and make sure students understand what is allowable and expected of them.

Large Sections

Many courses have high enrollments, making it necessary to create sections with 100 students or more. These sections are often taught in large auditoriums or lecture halls. A large section presents a different kind of learning experience that encompasses its own set of problems for faculty and students, such as the difficulty of using discussion or group methods with 150 or more students, assessing student learning in any form other than a multiple-choice exam, and interacting with students, especially when the instructor has to stand on a stage or raised platform and use a microphone to be seen and heard. Although these concerns are legitimate, they can be minimized by incorporating aspects of the teaching techniques outlined above. For example, faculty can intersperse questions throughout a learning experience, asking students from different sections of the room to respond. Instructors might also consider forming small discussion groups to encourage students to get to know each other and to share ideas and perspectives.

McKeachie (1994) confirms the importance of incorporating a variety of teaching techniques to keep students actively engaged. Instructors might consider using multiple role-playing activities or encouraging students to write on a note card two questions or facts about the material covered during each class session. Other recommendations to help increase learning in large sections include:

- Form discussion groups. Many group activities can occur in the discussion section. Periodic discussion section reports can be made by one group member during the whole class session.
- Make use of the classroom assessment techniques by Angelo and Cross (1993).
- Devise quick activities that encourage students to get to know each other so that students feel less isolated.

Understanding how to prepare for a large section can help you effectively meet the challenge of this type of learning environment. If you have just received your first large lecture teaching assignment, we suggest that you first talk to colleagues who have experience teaching large sections. Their guidance can help make your first experience successful for both you and your students.

Seminar Format

The seminar is one of the most commonly used teaching formats in higher education. Although generally considered an instructional format for upper-level students, the seminar is being used more and more at the lower levels to introduce research and presentation skills earlier in the education cycle. Seminars can be taught in a traditional classroom or in a conference room where the instructor and students sit around a large conference table. In contrast to large classes, these highly interactive sessions provide ample opportunity for using active learning teaching strategies, engaging both the instructor and the students in the learning process. As in most active learning environments, the faculty role is one of guide and monitor.

Technology

Today, educators realize that computer literacy is an important part of a student's education. Integrating technology into a course curriculum when appropriate is proving to be valuable for enhancing and extending the learning experience for faculty and students. Today's technologies offer many tools for teaching, such as word processing, spreadsheets, databases, electronic mail, interactive home pages, and Web-based conferencing. Many faculty have found electronic mail and course home pages on the World Wide Web to be useful ways to promote student-student or faculty-student communication about class meetings, discussion topics, or relevant on-line resources. Other instructors use list-serves or on-line notes to extend topic discussions and explore critical issues with students and colleagues.

Students come to us with varying degrees of computer literacy. Faculty who use technology regularly often find it necessary to provide some basic skill instruction during the first week of class. In the future, we expect that need to decline. A more detailed discussion about the use of technology, teaching, and learning is presented in Chapter 9, "Technology."

Distance Learning

Distance learning is not a new concept. We have all experienced learning outside of a structured classroom setting through television or correspondence courses. Distance learning or distance education as a teaching pedagogy, however, is an important topic of discussion on college campuses today. It is defined as "any form of teaching and learning in which the teacher and learner are not in the same place at the same time" (Gilbert, 1995, p. 3).

Information technology has broadened our concept of the learning environment. It has made it possible for learning experiences to be extended beyond the confines of the traditional classroom. Distance learning technologies take many forms, such as computer simulations, interactive collaboration and discussion, interactive videos, Web-based instruction, and the creation of virtual learning environments connecting regions or nations. To be successful, these kinds of teaching techniques require sufficient technical resources and support staff. Instructors should consult with their institution's technical support staff to determine the possibilities of using these kinds of teaching tools. Distance learning is covered in greater detail in Chapter 9, "Technology."

❖ THE COURSE

After you have thought about the behaviors and attitudes characteristic of exemplary teachers, considered the implications of the variety of learning styles that your students can be expected to bring to the learning experience, and considered the range of teaching methods and techniques available as you prepare to teach, it is time to put all the parts together in the form of a course. In developing a course, you must consider what you want to accomplish (*course objectives*), you must communicate your expectations to your students (*syllabus*), you must determine that your educational objectives have been met (*students' assignments and evaluations*), and you must reflect on the extent to which you have successfully accomplished your goals (*course and faculty assessment*). In this section, we address all these points.

Objectives

As you begin to develop a course, you must first think about the course type, level, and role within a curriculum. Depending on the circumstances, you may have considerable freedom to determine the content and objectives of the course, or you may be asked to teach a course for which the content and objectives have been determined for you, usually by a program or departmental committee. If the content and objectives have already been established for you, sample syllabi and assignments should be available from which you can develop your own version of the course. Assuming that the course you are developing is a new one and you are free to determine the content and objectives yourself, how do you get started? There are two questions to be concerned about:

1. What should the content of the course be?
2. What do you want your students to learn as a result of taking the course?

Sometimes there are textbooks available that will provide a good overview of the subject; in other cases, you can consult the syllabi of colleagues for a sense of what other professionals thought about the organization of the course. If you are dealing with a new course for which you do not have a model, it will be up to you to determine the course content and objectives. To determine the content of the course, you should start by brainstorming about all the possible topics and themes that might be covered under the heading of the course. After you have created an exhaustive list, begin to eliminate topics that you cannot or should not cover. To do this, you will need to develop some criteria for categorizing each topic. One way of determining what to include is assigning a value to each topic by answering the following questions (Lowman, 1995; Pregent, 1994):

- How essential is this topic to the content of the course?
- How essential is this skill for students' learning?
- How interesting will this topic be for students?
- How difficult will this topic be for students?

By assigning values to each topic using these criteria, you can begin to eliminate topics that you will not be able to cover. Remember that time is an important consideration in developing a course. The typical 3-credit course meets for 150 minutes each week over the course of 15 weeks. If the course meets three times a week, there will be 45 class meetings. Assuming that the first class is used for introductions and administrative purposes and that you use two other class periods for tests, you are left with 42 class meetings for actual instruction. The last question is closely associated with the time issue because the more difficult the topic is, the longer it will take the class to cover the material. For classes meeting once a week, such as graduate courses, there are special considerations stemming from the length of time between each meeting. Extra care should be given to the development of topics and the need to reiterate key points in subsequent meetings.

Answers to the first three questions are primarily a matter of determining the course objectives. The best way to think about objectives is to consider them to be a set of questions that you are asking about the material, about your students, about yourself, and about the combination of these in the learning experience. Remember that determining course objectives may not simply be a matter of what you want to cover. You must also consider the place of the course in the curriculum. For example, if the course is the first in a sequence, then the expectations of faculty teaching later in the sequence will help to determine the goals you set for what your students learn. Also, if the course satisfies general education requirements, there may be goals for the course in addition to any content objectives you set. For example, in a general education course, you might be expected to cover skills in problem solving, writing, or electronic communication in addition to any content goals related to, say, philosophy or history.

As you think about developing objectives for your course, consider that there are general and specific objectives (Pregent, 1994). General objectives are set from the perspective of the instructor. They depend in part on the course description and level, but they always involve educating students rather than covering topics (McKeachie, 1994). A statement of a general objective is brief—one to three lines—and includes a verb indicating what will be accomplished. For example, "introduce students to . . ." or "help students to develop the skill of. . . ."

In contrast, specific objectives, also short statements, are written from the perspective of the student. Specific objectives are also keyed to verbs and express what the student should know or be able to do at the conclusion of the course or course section (Lowman, 1995). Examples of specific objective statements are "list the features of . . . ," "explain the relevance of . . . ," "apply the theory to . . . ," "analyze the causes of . . . ," "design a plan for . . . ," and "evaluate the outcome of. . . ."

In developing course objectives, it is important to keep our earlier discussion of Bloom's (1956) taxonomy in mind. Remember that the cognitive domain has six levels, according to Bloom. Although a course may have objectives relating to several levels, one would expect a college course to provide significant learning experiences at the upper levels of the scale. Thus, although one might expect students to learn a certain number of facts in a course, one would also expect the course to demand a significant amount of analysis, synthesis, or evaluation. Finally, it is not sufficient simply to write course objectives that refer to the higher orders in the taxonomy. It is the instructor's responsibility to develop learning experiences that model the order of knowledge or skill students are expected to acquire and to develop course assignments that reinforce them.

Course Syllabus

All faculty should provide students with a printed syllabus during the first class meeting. A course syllabus is essentially a contract between the instructor and the student. It should contain a course description with clearly stated goals and objectives and an outline of course requirements for the students. Developing a syllabus gives you the opportunity to work out the implications of the decisions you have already made concerning the importance of the subject area topics in conjunction with their level of interest to the students and their level of difficulty (Pregent, 1994). The syllabus should contain a chronological listing of the topics to be covered and the activities associated with each topic. Usually, copies of previous course syllabi are available from academic unit administrative offices. A course syllabus should contain the components outlined in Table 2.4.

Table 2.4 Syllabus Components

Components	Description
General course information	Course number, title, semester Number of credits Instructor's name, office hours, office address, telephone number(s) and e-mail address, if applicable
Course description	Narrative description of course content
Course objectives	General objectives from the instructor's perspective Specific objectives from the student's perspective Link objectives to course materials
Course expectations	Be explicit about your policies concerning: • attendance • class preparation • participation • missed exams • assignment due dates • Honor Code requirements (if applicable)
Course texts and materials	List of required texts, including bibliographic information Course reading packets (if applicable) Any other course materials required for full participation
Course requirements	List all requirements and expectations (graded and ungraded) for completing the course. Describe assignments, including projects (individual or group), papers, examination. Provide information about format, length, degree of collaboration permitted, due dates.
Grading criteria	Provide a scale expressing relative weight or point distribution for each assignment or activity, including class participation. If participation will be graded, students need to know what will be counted in the participation grade.

Depending on local requirements or practices, other types of information may be included. For example, if your institution has an honor code, you may want to include a statement reminding students about their responsibility in maintaining the academic integrity of the learning process, and outline what constitutes a violation. Appendix 2.3 provides examples of both undergraduate (philosophy) and graduate (education) syllabi.

Lesson Plans

Faculty who are new to teaching or teaching a course for the first time may find it useful to develop lesson plans. Just as the syllabus represents the structure of the entire course, including a chronology, the lesson plan provides a structure for the individual class session. A lesson plan consists of an outline of the main topic(s) to be covered together with any subtopics associated with it. You should include an estimate of the time you wish to spend on each topic to be covered and the associated teaching technique you intend to use. The lesson plan should provide a review of the general and specific objectives you have set for the topic and the activities you have devised to ensure that the objectives are met. Having a detailed lesson plan gives you an opportunity to revisit the lesson after the class is completed. You may determine what worked and what did not and make notes for revision the next time that you give the lesson. Appendix 2.4 contains a sample lesson plan that incorporates several different teaching methods and techniques.

Assessing Student Work

Among the many tasks of a college teacher, probably none is approached with less enthusiasm than creating and grading student assignments. Most faculty do not perform this aspect of their responsibilities very well, perhaps because they consider testing to be an afterthought imposed by a society hung up on accreditation. A very different attitude might result if faculty saw testing and grading as an integral part of the learning experience. If you have stayed with us in this chapter through the discussions of exemplary teaching, learning styles, teaching methods, and course development, you have come to appreciate the importance of establishing course, unit, and lesson objectives. It is equally important to find out whether these objectives have been met by determining how well students understand the material you have covered. In this sense, giving and grading tests and other assignments are not extraneous additions; they are part of instruction.

Types of Graded Assignments

Exams and related assignments. There are many types of exams, including essay, matching, true-false, multiple choice, and short answer. In addition to traditional examination formats, faculty make use of a variety of assignments to determine the extent to which students have mastered the key points of a lesson or topic. Some alternative assignments and formats include the use of journals or portfolios, as well as student performances and presentations. The selection of exam type should be based on the learning objectives of the examination or assignment and the nature of the content covered.

Construction of an exam may seem simple on the surface, but experienced faculty know that every evaluation instrument is flawed to some degree. In addition to the type and content of an examination, a faculty member should consider the most appropriate format for conducting the examination. As Table 2.5 indicates, these can vary from the traditional in-class test to take-home examinations or group assignments. Assignments follow the same continuum as teaching methods—from the classic multiple-choice test or essay to the use of portfolios. Table 2.5 also presents the types of examinations and assignments most frequently used in higher education settings, along with the cognitive characteristics most often associated with each. The distinctions outlined in the table are not hard and fast, but they do provide a framework for you to think about as you choose the most appropriate type of assignment to accomplish your learning objectives.

Information technology is also having an effect on testing. Computers can be used as an alternative delivery system for the standard pencil and paper test, but the power of the computer can be used for more innovative testing. It is possible to develop a program that has the computer select questions from a large pool of items stored in its memory. The items are categorized by level of difficulty, and the computer selects increasingly more difficult items depending on the student's success in responding to each item. Such programs allow an instructor to monitor an individual student's command of the subject area. They also contribute to learner-centered approaches in education by allowing students to proceed through a topic at their own pace.

Many guides are available to help faculty in the construction of exams such as those that accompany faculty editions of textbooks. Be sure to ask your textbook representative about other available resources. Don't hesitate to seek assistance in this area. Fair and equitable assessment of student learning should be a top priority. Once students have completed

Table 2.5 Assignment Types and Characteristics

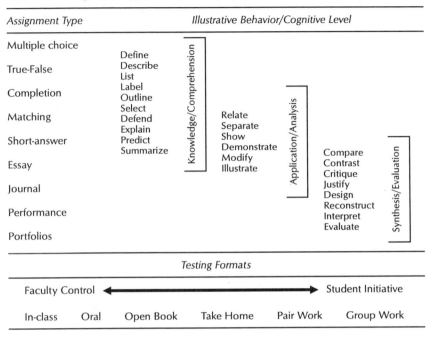

Assignment Type	Illustrative Behavior/Cognitive Level

Multiple choice

True-False

Completion

Matching

Short-answer

Essay

Journal

Performance

Portfolios

Define
Describe
List
Label
Outline
Select
Defend
Explain
Predict
Summarize

Knowledge/Comprehension

Relate
Separate
Show
Demonstrate
Modify
Illustrate

Application/Analysis

Compare
Contrast
Critique
Justify
Design
Reconstruct
Interpret
Evaluate

Synthesis/Evaluation

Testing Formats

Faculty Control ◄──────────► Student Initiative

In-class   Oral   Open Book   Take Home   Pair Work   Group Work

an exam, grade it and return it to them as soon as possible. Some of the most effective student learning occurs after an exam.

Group work. As more faculty integrate active learning strategies into their course design, issues about grading group work become critical. If you use some form of group work in your course, be sure students know which assignments involve group effort and which are to be done individually. In addition, be clear about evaluation criteria. If students are graded as a group, establish how the grade will be determined. Will each student in the group receive the same grade? How will the instructor distribute the workload in the group assignment to ensure that each student contributes equally? If each student within a group is to receive an individual grade, what criteria are used to make the assessment? Many group conflicts stem from students' perceptions that the workload is not evenly distributed. One way of dealing with this is to ask each member of a group to assess all other members of the group. Design group assignments to ensure that each member participates equally. We recommend that assignment descriptions clearly outline the degree of collaboration expected and how student effort will be evaluated.

Participation. Involving students in the learning process means that students need to come to class prepared to participate. Recognizing that participation is an important course expectation, most course syllabi include participation as a component of the final grade. Too often, however, the criteria used to evaluate participation are not articulated. Because participation often makes up 10% to 20% of a student's course grade, we recommend that syllabi clearly outline the requirements necessary to receive full participation credit and how those judgments will be made. One of the most frequent sources of student complaints about grading stems from unclear or unstated criteria for assessing a student's class participation effort.

Written work. Grading written work is not only time-consuming, it is often seen as subjective by students. To help counter the issue of subjective grading, faculty may want to (1) provide students with guidelines and examples, if possible, of their expectations for each written assignment, and (2) give students detailed written feedback about what they did well and how they could improve. Appendix 2.5 provides an example of the grading criteria for a paper.

Assessing the Course and Your Teaching

When the goal is maximizing learning, it is important to monitor regularly the progress of the course and your teaching. Most colleges and universities now use some form of student evaluation for courses; however, because the evaluations are usually administered at the end of the semester, the results are not available to the faculty member until after the semester is over. Although this information may be useful for revising the course for future offerings, the faculty member doesn't have anything to use while the course is being taught. One way of describing end-of-semester evaluations is to say that they focus on the teacher and the course. Most evaluations of this type are designed to elicit a global, summative evaluation from students about the quality of the course and the faculty member's instruction. In some cases, the form may include additional questions that ask for students' opinions about various elements of the course. On the basis of responses to these questions, faculty might have sufficient information to improve the course. For the most part, however, end-of-semester evaluations are not very good devices for getting students and faculty to observe the learning process with the goal of improving it. Appendix 2.6 provides a typical course evaluation form.

Recently, because of the work of Patricia Cross and Thomas Angelo (1993), faculty have begun to see the benefits of periodically focusing on the effectiveness of the course and instructional techniques by asking students to respond to questions that get at their attitudes about the course and their understanding of the course material (B. Davis, 1993). They call their strategies for periodic data gathering about the success of the learning experiences "classroom assessment techniques." Regular use of these allows the faculty member to ask three important questions continually concerning the course:

- What are the knowledge and skills I am trying to teach?
- How well are the students learning what I am trying to teach?
- How can I help my students learn better?

Most faculty have had the disappointing experience of assuming that students were learning what was being taught only to discover by grading an exam or assignment that the students understood very little of what was covered. Classroom assessment techniques allow the faculty member to monitor student understanding and attitudes.

The teacher decides what, when, and how to assess the course or lesson. Perhaps most important, by responding to the information received from students and making adjustments to the tone or content of the course, the faculty member remains in charge of the learning experience. At the same time, by consulting students about how the course is proceeding and how well they understand the material, faculty allow students to remain engaged in the course. For this reason, it is important to share the results of the assessment with the class. Reporting how the class responded and what actions you are taking as a result of the information you received is clear evidence that you care about their opinions and value their suggestions. At times, you may not have control over the problem bothering students, such as a classroom in poor condition; however, explaining what you can and cannot do about the situation is important for class morale.

When and how often classroom assessment should take place is a judgment call by the faculty member. We can offer some general guidelines. If you are teaching a new course for the first time, it is useful to get an early reading on how well things are going. In this case, surveying students after the first 3 or 4 weeks of the semester is recommended. If the course is one you have taught often, it is probably sufficient to wait until the midpoint of the semester and then make corrections if necessary. Of course, staying aware of student reactions throughout the course is important so that you can try to adjust whenever something goes awry.

Classroom assessment techniques are used to get information about two types of issues: (1) students' attitude toward the course, and (2) how much students have understood. A simple way to get information about your students' reactions to the course is to hand out blank index cards during the last 10 minutes of a session. Ask students to list the two or three things they like most about the course on one side of the card; ask students to list the two or three things that have caused them difficulty and should be improved on the other side of the card. Also ask them to provide suggestions for making improvements (Pregent, 1994). By using the index cards, you can sort the responses quickly and determine the extent to which things are or are not working.

A similar device can be used to determine the extent to which students have understood the material you have covered. At the conclusion of an important segment, distribute index cards and ask students to tell you on one side the two most important points made during the lecture or discussion. Ask students to list the points they still do not understand or about which they are having the most difficulty on the other side of the card. This strategy has become very popular and has come to be called the "1-minute paper" or "minute paper," though, in practice, it takes a little longer than 1 minute to accomplish.

The product of most classroom assessment techniques is a piece of writing by students, so it is possible to combine course assessment with other pedagogical objectives. In addition, there are other ways to gather the information. For example, you could engage in a full class discussion of course-related issues or meet with students designated by their classmates to speak on their behalf. If you have a colleague who is willing, your colleague could interview your students and give you a report that preserves student anonymity. Angelo and Cross (1993) discuss 50 different strategies that they group by category. The categories include course-related knowledge and skills; learner attitudes, values, and self awareness; and learner reactions to instruction. Barbara Davis (1993, pp. 345-353) also summarizes a variety of techniques gathered from a number of sources. It is useful to vary the techniques you use to solicit student reaction. Whatever techniques you use, you will find that your students remain more engaged in the learning process.

❖ NOTE

1. Bloom's (1956) taxonomy is one of the most widely recognized schemas of cognitive development. There are other ways of viewing human cognitive development. Among these are Holland's (1966) typology of personality and Kolb's (1984) model of experimental learning.

❖ REFERENCES

Angelo, T. A., & Cross, K. P. (1993). _Classroom assessment techniques: A handbook for college teachers_ (2nd ed.). San Francisco: Jossey-Bass.

Barbe, W., & Swassing, R. (1979). _Teaching through modality strengths: Concepts and practices._ Columbus, OH: Zaner-Bloser.

Bloom, B. S. (1956). _Taxonomy of educational objectives: Book 1 cognitive domain._ New York: Longman.

Bridges, C. M., Ware, W. B., Brown, B. B., & Greenwood, G. (1971). Characteristics of best and worst college teachers. _Science Education, 55,_ 543-553.

Bruffee, K. A. (1993). _Collaborative learning: Higher education, interdependence, and the authority of knowledge._ Baltimore: Johns Hopkins University Press.

Centra, J. A. (1993). _Reflective faculty evaluation._ San Francisco: Jossey-Bass.

Claxton, C. S., & Murrell, P. H. (1987). _Learning styles: Implications for improving educational practices_ (ASHE-ERIC Higher Education Report No. 4). Washington, DC: Association for the Study of Higher Education.

Cohen, P. A. (1981). Student ratings of instruction and student achievement. _Review of Educational Research, 51,_ 281-309.

Cuseo, J. (1992). Collaborative & cooperative learning in higher education: A proposed taxonomy. _Cooperative Learning and College Teaching, 2_(2), 2-4.

Davis, B. G. (1993). _Tools for teaching._ San Francisco: Jossey-Bass.

Davis, J. R. (1993). _Better teaching, more learning._ Phoenix, AZ: Oryx.

Eble, K. E. (1982). _The craft of teaching._ San Francisco: Jossey-Bass.

Epstein, J. (1981). *Masters: Portraits of great teachers*. New York: Basic Books.

Feldman, K. A. (1976). The superior college teacher from the students' view. *Research in Higher Education, 5*, 243-288.

Feldman, K. A. (1988). Effective college teaching from the students' and faculty's view: Matched or mismatched priorities? *Research in Higher Education, 28*, 291-344.

Gabbert, B., Johnson, D. W., & Johnson, R. (1986). Cooperative learning, group-to-individual transfer, process gain, and the acquisition of cognitive reasoning strategies. *Journal of Psychology, 120*(3), 265-278.

Gilbert, S. W. (1995). Why distance education? *AAHE Bulletin, 48*, 4.

Grasha, A. F. (1984). Learning styles: The journey from Greenwich observatory (1796) to the college classroom (1984). *Improving College and University Teaching, 32*, 1.

Halpern, D. F. (1996). *Thought and knowledge: An introduction to critical thinking* (3rd ed.). Mahwah, NJ: Lawrence Erlbaum.

Hartley, J., & Davies, I. K. (1978). Note-taking: A critical review. *Programmed Learning and Educational Technology, 15*, 207-224.

Holland, J. L. (1966). *The psychology of vocational choice*. Waltham, MA: Ginn.

Hyman, R. T. (1974). *Ways of teaching* (2nd ed.). New York: Lippincott.

Johnson, D. W., & Johnson, R. T. (1995). *Creative controversy: Intellectual challenge in the classroom*. Edina, MN: Interaction.

Johnson, D. W., Johnson, R. T., & Holubec, E. J. (1993). *Cooperation in the classroom*. Edina, MN: Interaction.

Johnson, D. W., Johnson, R. T., & Smith, K. A. (1991). *Active learning: Cooperation in the college classroom*. Edina, MN: Interaction.

Kolb, D. A. (1984). *Experiential learning: Experience as the source of learning and development*. New York: Prentice Hall.

Lowman, J. (1995). *Mastering the techniques of teaching* (2nd ed.). San Francisco: Jossey-Bass.

McKeachie, W. (1994). *Teaching tips: A guidebook for the beginning college teacher* (9th ed.). Boston: D.C. Heath.

Messick, S., & Associates. (1976). *Individuality in learning*. San Francisco: Jossey-Bass.

Meyers, C., & Jones, T. B. (1993). *Promoting active learning: Strategies for the college classroom*. San Francisco: Jossey-Bass.

Millis, B. J. (1994). Conducting cooperative cases: To improve the academy: Resources for faculty, students, and institutional development. *Professional & Organizational Development Network in Higher Education, 13*, 308-329.

Millis, B. J. (1996). Connecting with cooperative learning. In V. Bianco-Mathis & N. Chalofsky (Eds.), *The adjunct faculty handbook* (pp. 115-131). Thousand Oaks, CA: Sage.

Millis, B. J., & Cottell, P. G., Jr. (1998). *Cooperative learning for higher education*. Phoenix, AZ: Oryx.

Myers, I., & McCaulley, M. (1985). *Manual: A guide to the development and use of the Myers-Briggs type indicator*. Palo Alto, CA: Consulting Psychologists Press.

Pregent, R. (1994). *Charting your course: How to prepare to teach more effectively*. Madison, WI: Magna.

Sagan, C. (1977). *The dragons of Eden*. New York: Ballantine.

Seldin, P. (1994). *Changing practices in faculty evaluation*. San Francisco: Jossey-Bass.

Sherman, T. M., et al. (1987). The quest for excellence in university teaching. *Journal of Higher Education, 58*, 66-84.

Skon, L., Johnson, D. W., & Johnson, R. (1981). Cooperative peer interaction versus individual competition and individualistic efforts: Effects on the acquisition of cognitive reasoning strategies. *Journal of Educational Psychology, 73*(1), 83-92.

Smith, B. L., & MacGregor, J. T. (1992). What is cooperative learning? In A. Goodsell, M. Mahler, V. Tinto, B. L. Smith, & J. MacGregor (Eds.), *Collaborative learning: A sourcebook for higher education* (pp. 9-22). University Park, PA: National Center on Postsecondary Teaching, Learning, and Assessment.

Appendix 2.1

Considerations for Preparing Lectures

Preparation

- Consider your audience and course level.
- Carefully select materials that relate to the lesson topic.
- Be realistic about what you can effectively cover; do not attempt to cover more than five major points in a 50-minute period.
- Break up the lecture by using a variety of activities to keep students involved, such as posing questions, asking each student to explain a lesson concept to another student in the class, or asking students to write one example describing how they might use a key concept in their own lives.
- Create an outline and share it with your students by writing the outline on a blackboard, whiteboard, or overhead transparency.
- Avoid reading a prepared script. Present your lecture from note cards or an outline.
- Rehearse your lecture so that you feel comfortable and speak naturally.

Presentation

- Use themes that show students connections between the lesson and the other parts of the course.
- Provide examples and illustrations that your students will understand and relate to.
- Be attentive to your audience, recognizing when you need to slow down, insert an interesting story, or use a new technique to reengage your students.
- Vary your speech patterns.
- Try not to be rooted to one spot; move around the room.
- Divide the lecture into manageable intervals by pausing to ask questions or involving students in some task.
- Be enthusiastic about your topic and excited about teaching.
- Repeat key points several times during the lecture.
- End your lecture with a summary.

Assessment

- Ask questions about the material just covered, giving students from each section of the room an opportunity to think and respond.
- Ask students to note difficult points that need clarification. Collect the information, review it before the next session, and begin the next session by addressing as many of them as possible.

Appendix 2.2

Sample Collaborative Learning Scenarios

Scenario 1: Using Groups to Enhance Understanding of Course Readings

Faced with increasing numbers of complaints from students about the difficulty of the primary sources assigned for the course, a philosophy professor teaching an introductory course in ethical theory decided to try using groups to help students understand the course readings. The groups are formed at the second class meeting and remain together for the entire semester. For the purpose of this course, it is important that there be as much diversity as possible, so the professor assigns students to groups randomly using birth months. Some adjustments may be made to ensure gender and ethnic diversity. The enrollment for the course is set at 35, so there are usually six groups, each having up to six students. In addition to the groups, the professor uses an electronic list-serve to communicate with the students and to provide them with an avenue for asking questions about the readings or to pursue an electronic discussion of an issue that arose from the readings or the in-class discussion. Readings in primary sources are assigned to each topic in the course. Approximately 1 week before the start of a new topic, the professor posts a set of six questions on the list-serve to guide the students to and through the main points of the reading (early in the semester, while students are trying to enroll in the class, a handout of the questions is also provided). Students are expected to read the primary source prior to the first class on the topic and to outline a response to each of the six questions. During class meetings, students work in groups; each group is assigned one of the questions by the professor. Students spend approximately 20 to 25 minutes discussing the reading and developing an appropriate response to the question. In the process, students become peer teachers. The roles of reporter, recorder, and facilitator are rotated to different members of the group for each new set of questions to ensure that everyone is participating. During the class meeting, the professor visits each group to assist in its deliberation as needed. At the end of the discussion period, each group reports to the class on the answer to its assigned question. The issue is then open for general class discussion.

Scenario 2: Using Groups to Undertake Research Projects

Because students are usually unfamiliar and apprehensive about research methodologies, a professor in a graduate education research course establishes groups for undertaking a collaborative research study. The groups are formed during the third class meeting after students have had an opportunity to get to know each other and have learned about each others' research interests. Teams of five are formed based on their willingness to undertake a particular research project. The project requires a literature review, creation of a research instrument, data collection, analyses of quantitative and qualitative data, synthesis, evaluation, and conclusion (see Appendixes 2.3 and 2.5 for reference to this assignment in a sample syllabus and for grading criteria). Specific assignments are given to each member of the group to ensure that each contributes equally to the completion of the study. In addition to performing each assigned task, members are expected to discuss what is involved in accomplishing each step and to help one another resolve difficulties that arise. In this manner, group members serve as peer teachers of some of the more difficult aspects of the research process. For example, through using groups, students seem to have a better understanding of basic statistical analyses and how statistics contribute to understanding the research question. To accomplish the group project successfully, members must be willing to work cooperatively and to share group responsibilities. The project involves both in-class and out-of-class tasks and is distributed over 12 weeks of the 15-week semester. The professor serves as a facilitator, resource, and guide as the groups move through the research process.

Appendix 2.3

Sample Syllabi

We have provided two sample syllabi. The first, *Introduction to Ethics,* is a lower-level course in the humanities; the second, *Introduction to Educational Research,* is a masters-level research course.

PHILOSOPHY 151, 001
INTRODUCTION TO ETHICS
Tues., Thurs. 9:00-10:15
Spring, 1997

Dr. James J. Fletcher
Office: East Bldg. 125
Phone: 993-8775
Office Hours: Tues. & Thurs., 10:30-Noon
E-mail: jfletche@osf1.gmu.edu
Course Listserv: PHIL151-001@gmu.edu

Last date to drop course without incurring a grade of F: 5pm, Friday, February 21.

Course Description: An examination of classic and contemporary ethical theories, including virtue ethics, utilitarianism, deontology, and care. The course will explore such issues as definitions of *good* and *happiness,* the nature of the good life, decision procedures for determining right actions, and applications to real-life problems.
(3 credits)

Course Objectives:

General Objectives:
1. To explain the unique features of ethical arguments
2. To explore the dominant moral theories in western philosophy
3. To examine the application of ethical theories to some current moral problems
4. To provide opportunities for collaborative learning through groups and electronic communication

Specific Objectives:

Students will be able to
1. Identify and apply the components of ethical arguments
2. Recognize the characteristic features of western moral theories
3. Begin the process of ethical analysis
4. Apply ethical theories to moral problems or issues

5. Write clearly about moral issues and problems
6. Participate actively in group discussions
7. Achieve facility in the use of electronic communication

Texts—Required:

D. T. Goldberg, *Ethical Theory and Social Issues,* Second Edition, Harcourt Brace, 1995.

Course Reading Packet (available at the Copy Center in Johnson Learning Center). The packet contains the following readings:

Katie G. Cannon, "Moral Wisdom in the Black Women's Literary Tradition"
Joseph Ellin, "Challenges to Ethics: Egoism"
Carol Gilligan, "Moral Orientation and Moral Development"
L. M. Hinman, "The Ethics of Diversity: Gender, Ethnicity, and Individuality"
Barbara MacKinnon, "Ethical Relativism"
Plato, "Myth of Gyges," from *The Republic*
Vincent Ruggiero, "Comparing Cultures"
Cornel West, "Nihilism in Black America" from *Race Matters*
Thomas White, "Ethics: What It Is, Does, and Isn't"

Course Methods: The primary method of instruction will be through small group discussions supplemented by lecture. In the belief that the depth of your learning is dependent on the extent of your involvement, we will make heavy use of small group discussions and reports. E-mail exchanges will also be an essential part of the course.

Expectations: Although there is no direct connection between class attendance and grades, you cannot achieve your involvement in the learning process unless you participate fully in the class discussions. Your participation in the small group discussions is especially critical. The other members of your group may be asked to assess your contribution to the group. *It should be obvious that you cannot contribute to the class or to your group if you have not prepared the readings prior to class, if you are chronically late, or if you fail to attend class on the discussion days.* You will also be expected to contribute to class discussions on the list-serve. At least one contribution per week is the norm. Your participation grade will be based on your contributions to the class, group, and electronic discussions. *All assignments must be submitted at the start of the class on the scheduled date. Late work will be penalized one grade for each day beyond the deadline. Makeup examinations are rarely given and only for extraordinary circumstances beyond your control, such as a grave illness or family emergency. Written documentation is required.*

Honor Code: You are encouraged to discuss the course with others and to work together in preparation for class meetings. All of your written work, however, is to be yours alone. Remember that plagiarism is a violation of the honor code; if you use the ideas or opinions of others in quotation or paraphrase, you must identify your sources and provide citations.

Assignments:

1. In-class exams (2)   40%
2. Position paper (1)   20%
3. Final examination   30%
4. Class participation   10%

Schedule: (Course Topics and Assignments)

Week	Dates	Topic	Readings
1-3		*Part I: Introduction*	
	1/21, 1/23	Introduction	
		Readings:	Goldberg, Gen Intro., pp. 1-7.
			White, "Ethics: What It Is . . . "
	1/28	Egoism	
		Readings:	Ellin, "Challenges to Ethics: Egoism"
			Plato, "Myth of Gyges"
	1/30	Relativism	
		Readings:	MacKinnon, "Ethical Relativism"
			Ruggiero, "Comparing Cultures"
	2/4, 2/6	Overview of Theories	
		Readings:	Goldberg, pp. 27-29, 188-189,
			197-198; 56-58, 64-66; 82-83,
			91-95; 116-117, 126-129; 148-149,
			169-170, 180; 213-215.
4-13		*Part II: Moral Theories*	
	2/11-2/18		Aristotle—Ethics as Virtue: Character
		Readings:	Goldberg, pp. 27-41, 52-54.
	2/20	**First Test (Egoism, Relativism, Virtue Ethics)**	
	2/25-3/6	Utilitarianism—Pursuit of Happiness:	
			Bentham and Mill
		Readings:	Goldberg, pp. 116-121, 124-126,
			126-142.
8	**3/11-3/13**	**Spring Break—No Class**	
	3/18	**Position Paper due no later than today**	
	3/18-4/1		Kant—Deontology: Duty
		Readings:	Goldberg, pp. 91-113.
	4/2	**Second Exam (Utilitarians and Kant)**	
	4/8-4/17		Other Voices: Gender and Ethnicity
		Readings:	Goldberg, pp. 213-223, Hinman,
			Gilligan, Cannon, and West
14-15	4/22-5/1	*Part III: Contemporary Moral Issues*	
		Moral Issues to be chosen in class from the	
		selections in Goldberg.	

5/13   **Tuesday, May 13th, 7:30-10:15 am**
                  Final Examination

EDRS 590, Methods of Educational Research
SECTION 004 (WED 7:20-10:00)
Spring 1997
ROBINSON A352

Sondra Patrick, Ph.D.
East Building, Room 125
993-8775/8790(w); 250-7335(h)
WED 6:00-7:00 p.m. or by appointment
spatrick@gmu.edu

COURSE DESCRIPTION

Develops skills, insights, and understandings basic to performing research, with emphasis on interpretation and application of research results. The course examines research methodologies research and applies them to educational settings.

COURSE OBJECTIVES

General Objectives

1. To develop proficient users of educational research.
2. To familiarize students with the application of technology to educational research.
3. To assist students in acquiring the ability to read and understand research articles.

Specific Objectives

1. To be able to critically read and analyze quantitative and qualitative research studies in their field of instruction.
2. To recognize various types of research designs and the application of each to educational settings.
3. To understand and use research methodology in conducting research studies.
4. To construct a simple survey instrument and use basic scanning programs to process data.
5. To use descriptive statistics in analyzing research data.
6. To use inferential statistics in analyzing research data.
7. To use computers to process and analyze research data.
8. To research, write, and conduct a research project based on present educational problems, methods, and other appropriate concerns.
9. To recognize the opportunities for teachers to conduct research in educational settings.

COURSE FORMAT

The course will be divided into three segments. The first segment will provide an overview of the research process and illustrate some previous research projects. The second segment will demonstrate how to use computers to do both descriptive and inferential statistics. Designing survey instruments and scanning programs will also be covered. The final segment will provide class time for students to work on individual research projects. Computer labs will be available to conduct data analysis and scoring.

Reading the text before class can help you better understand concepts and procedures presented during class. You need to read the text!!! Class meetings will combine discussions (both small and large groups) with lectures when needed to add new material or explain more difficult concepts or procedures.

COURSE MATERIALS

L. R. Gay, *Educational Research: Competencies for Analysis and Application.* (5th edition) Columbus, OH: Merrill. **REQUIRED**

COURSE PACKET. Note: These items are available from the copy center in Room 117, Johnson Center. They are required for success in this course. The materials contain all lecture notes and lab work sheets. Information about lab computer programs is also included.

STAT-STAR COMPUTER PROGRAM is available in the University Bookstore. **OPTIONAL**

MICROTEST COMPUTER PROGRAM is provided for you in the computer lab classroom (A352) and in some Robinson I and Science & Tech I computer labs. You will be required to use the Microtest Survey Program to process and analyze your survey data. The Stat-Star program will be used to do the statistical analysis for your group project and lab work sheets.

Two 3.5 double-sided, high-density blank disks.

COURSE SCHEDULE

CLASS 1. INTRODUCTION TO COURSE/OVERVIEW OF SYLLABUS AND COURSE PROJECT. Class time to get instructor handouts. Lecture topics: Research methods and classifications. Read Chapters 1 and 2 to reinforce lecture.

CLASS 2. QUANTITATIVE AND QUALITATIVE RESEARCH METHODS/ SAMPLING/DEVELOPING HYPOTHESES AND RESEARCH QUESTIONS/ LINKING INFORMATION TO COURSE PROJECT. Read Chapter 7.

CLASS 3. DESCRIPTIVE STATISTICS LECTURE/RELIABILITY & VALIDITY. STAT-STAR introduction and Descriptive worksheet. Chapters 9, 12, & 13 will be covered during this class. You are to bring two **3.5 double-sided, high-density disks to class!!!!!**

CLASS 4. SAMPLING & INFERENTIAL STATISTICS LECTURE. STAT-STAR and Inferential worksheet. Read Chapter 14.

CLASS 5. OVERVIEW OF A QUANTITATIVE RESEARCH PROJECT/SAMPLING PROCEDURES/WRITING SURVEY QUESTIONS. Groups will also be formed during this session. Read Chapter 4.

CLASS 6. REVIEW DESCRIPTIVE & INFERENTIAL STATISTICS/REVIEW A QUANTITATIVE ARTICLE/COMPUTER LAB TIME.

CLASS 7. QUALITATIVE RESEARCH METHODS/WRITING OPEN-ENDED QUESTIONS/REVIEW A QUALITATIVE ARTICLE. Read Chapter 7.

CLASS 8. MID-TERM EXAM (first half of class). Second half of class—Discuss Group Project/NCSS Demonstration. The class will be instructed on how to use the MICROTEST Survey Software. This computer program will be used for printing, processing, and tabulating information related to your survey questionnaire. Read Chapter 5.

CLASS 9. SURVEY INSTRUMENT DEVELOPMENT/PRINTING/GROUP WORK. Each group will complete the development of a survey instrument. Have your work approved by the instructor before you print the information on your final scan forms. This will allow you **1 WEEK** for data collection.

CLASS 10. SURVEY SCORING NIGHT . . . PLEASE HAVE ALL YOUR FORMS COMPLETED BY THIS CLASS SESSION. GROUP WORK IN LAB. Time sheet for scanning will be made available. Your group will sign up for a scanning time.

CLASS 11. DATA COLLECTION EXPERIENCES. DATA ANALYSIS NIGHT. Students will use the NCS Program and Stat-Star to complete analysis of survey information.

CLASS 12. RESEARCH PROJECT UPDATES/EXPERIENCES. Read Chapter 5.

CLASS 13. WRITING RESEARCH REPORTS. The second-half of the class will be devoted to group work in the computer lab, etc. Read Chapters 8, 10, & 11.

CLASS 14. COMPUTER LAB TIME/FINISHING RESEARCH PROJECT.

CLASS 15. PROJECT REPORTS/FINAL PROJECTS DUE. NO LATE PROJECTS!

COURSE ASSIGNMENTS

RESEARCH PAPER PROJECT: POINT VALUE = 120

The research project for this course will be a group project. The class will be divided into five or six research groups. Each group will conduct a research project using both quantitative and qualitative data collection and data analysis. Groups will be formed early in the semester so that your research design can be developed throughout the first half of the course and implemented during the second half of the course.

MIDTERM EXAM: POINT VALUE = 60

The midterm exam will be a multiple-choice in-class exam. It will consist of 60 multiple choice questions taken from the text and material covered during the previous classes. Most of the questions will center on the lectures, instructor's handout, text, and text articles.

GRADES

Grades tend to be the focus of a significant amount of student concern. Although important, they should not be your major concern. "You know what you know," and the grade I record won't change that important fact. I suggest concentrating on learning and the grade will take care of itself. I am always willing to discuss this issue.

GRADE AND ASSOCIATED POINT VALUES

    A = 170 TO 200
    B = 145 TO 169
    C = LESS THAN 145

Grades will be based on three course components:

Group Research Project	120 points
Midterm Exam	60 points
In-Class + Group Participation	20 points
	200 points

Appendix 2.4

Sample Lesson Plan

Lesson Title: Challenges to Ethics: Egoism

This lesson is for a 100-level philosophy course introducing students to ethical theory (see Appendix 2.3 for the syllabus for this course). This is one of two lessons (the other is relativism) that looks at challenges to the assumptions underlying ethical theories. The main purpose of the lesson is to give a broad overview of egoism and the implications for ethics if egoism is true.

Class time: 1 75-minute class meeting.

Lesson Objectives:

General Objectives:

1. To explain the essential features of egoism
2. To distinguish psychological egoism from ethical egoism
3. To explore the differences between egoism and conventional morality
4. To continue the process of learning to analyze a philosophical text

Specific Objectives:

1. Students will be able to distinguish among egoism, altruism, and universalism.
2. Students will understand the difference between psychological egoism and ethical egoism and the logical relationship between them.
3. Students will realize that the basic premise of psychological egoism is incompatible with the demand of conventional morality and that one must occasionally sacrifice one's own interest when it is right to do so.

Readings:

Ellin, "Challenges to Ethics: Egoism," in Course Reading Packet.
Plato, "Myth of Gyges," from *The Republic,* in Course Reading Packet

Assignment:

Complete the Ellin and Plato readings before class.
Answer the questions posted on the list-serve about each reading. The questions serve as a guide to the main points students should get from the readings.

Class Activities:

1. Whole class discussion of the Myth of Gyges—15 minutes
2. Small group discussion of assigned questions—20 minutes
3. Group reports on answers to questions—25 minutes
4. Minilecture using PowerPoint overheads to summarize main points—15 minutes

Appendix 2.5

Sample Paper Assignment With Grading Criteria

The sample assignment presented here is taken from a master's-level research course in education (see Appendix 2.3 for the course syllabus). The paper is a group assignment: Each member of the group receives the same grade for the completed paper. Although no specific page limit is set, the average length is between 25 and 30 pages. In preparation for writing the paper, this assignment requires a literature review, quantitative and qualitative data analyses, and a reflection on the application of the methodology to the research question.

RESEARCH PAPER PROJECT: POINT VALUE = 120

The research project for this course will be a group project. The class will be divided into five or six research groups. Each group will conduct a research project using both quantitative and qualitative data collection and data analysis. Groups will be formed early in the semester so that your research design can be developed throughout the first half of the course and implemented during the second half of the course.

QUANTITATIVE PROJECT REQUIREMENTS:

1. Select a group topic and write the appropriate number of survey questions to fit a 5-point Likert-type scale.
2. Select three variables to test (age, gender, occupation, etc.). Each member of the group should contribute to the analysis of these variables. One of the variables must have three levels. Example: AGE (20-30) (31-50) (over 51).
3. A null hypothesis should be written for the various combinations of questions and variables.
4. The total group will assemble the survey instrument and print enough copies for each member to distribute. Each variable must have a minimum of 20 respondents per level. Example: Gender: 20 males and 20 females. Age: 20 teachers under 35 and 20 teachers over 36. The survey groups don't have to be equal, but should have a minimum of 20. In most cases, a larger respondent pool is better.
5. The forms will be collected by the group leader and brought to class for processing.
6. The raw data from the scanned forms will be copied to a disk to be analyzed. This will form the basis for the group's final report. You will use both the Microtest and Stat-Star computer programs for your data analysis.

QUALITATIVE RESEARCH REQUIREMENTS:

1. Each group will write three open-ended questions to accompany the survey. These will be printed on the back of the survey form. Respondents will write their responses to these open-ended questions when they complete the Likert-type scale survey.
2. The responses to the open-ended questions will be analyzed by looking for emerging themes and patterns in the words or phrases subjects write.

LITERATURE REVIEW:

1. Each member of a group should review one appropriate article and include a brief synopsis in the literature review section of the final written report. If possible, half the group should contribute an appropriate qualitative article and half should contribute an appropriate quantitative article.

FINAL WRITTEN REPORT:

POINT VALUE FOR EACH SECTION OF THE FINAL REPORT

INTRODUCTION (Overall Format)	5
LITERATURE REVIEW	5
QUANTITATIVE SECTION	
Statement of Hypotheses	10
Explanation of Procedures & Method	10
Analysis of Data	
Descriptive	20
Inferential	20
QUALITATIVE SECTION	
Statement of Open-Ended Questions	10
Explanation of Procedures & Method	10
Analysis of Contextual Data	10
CONCLUSIONS/RECOMMENDATIONS	10
APPENDIXES	
Survey Instrument	5
NCSS/STAT-STAR Printouts	5
TOTAL	120

Appendix 2.6

Sample Course and Faculty Evaluations
Student Questionnaire: Report on Teaching*

Instructor: _____   Course: _____   Date: _____

Pease take a few minutes to seriously consider and complete this form. It will be used to compile a Student Report on Teaching, which will be used as a part of the regular process of faculty evaluation. Space is provided on this report form for optional items selected by the department of the faculty member.

Your response to each item below should be a number from 5 to 1, or you may leave the item blank if you are unable to respond or feel that the item does not apply. Rate each item according to the following scale.

STRONGLY AGREE   5   4   3   2   1   STRONGLY DISAGREE

Place your rating in the space to the left of each statement

Course

_____ 1. The objectives of this course were made clear.
_____ 2. My course responsibilities were clearly defined.
_____ 3. The teaching materials required for this course were helpful.
_____ 4. The methods of evaluation (examinations, papers, projects, class discussions) were relevant and representative of the total course content.
_____ 5. I have been graded fairly and accurately.
_____ 6. Overall, the course was of value to me.

Instructor

_____ 7. The instructor's classroom sessions were stimulating.
_____ 8. The instructor showed enthusiasm for the subject.
_____ 9. The instructor communicated the subject matter effectively.
_____ 10. The instructor was well prepared for class.
_____ 11. The instructor encouraged and was responsive to student participation.
_____ 12. The instructor made adequate provisions for consultation and assistance.
_____ 13. The instructor showed an interest in and respect for me as an individual.
_____ 14. I would recommend this instructor to other students.
_____ 15. I would rate the instructor as an excellent teacher.

COMMENT ITEMS
16. Describe strengths of this class and/or instructor; try to be specific; use examples.

_____

_____

17. Describe weaknesses of this class and/or instructor; try to be specific; use examples.

_____

_____

18. What changes would you recommend for this class and/or instructor?

_____

_____

Any other comments?

_____

_____

Student Report on Instruction

Faculty member: _____ Term: _____

Course: _____ Department: _____

Please indicate your appraisal of the instructor's performance in this class by drawing a circle around the number that most closely expresses your view. Do not sign your name. Your thoughtful attention to the items on this form is sincerely appreciated.

	Strongly Agree			Strongly Disagree		Don't Know
1. The objectives of this course were clearly explained.	1	2	3	4	5	X
2. In-class activities were relevant to the objectives of the course.	1	2	3	4	5	X
3. The instructor was well prepared for class sessions.	1	2	3	4	5	X
4. The grading system was a fair way to measure knowledge/ability.	1	2	3	4	5	X
5. This course aroused my curiosity and challenged me intellectually.	1	2	3	4	5	X
6. The instructor was helpful when students had difficulty with course material.	1	2	3	4	5	X
7. The instructor was available and willing to consult with students during office hours.	1	2	3	4	5	X

OVERALL EVALUATION

8. The instructor was one of the best I have had at this college.	1	2	3	4	5	X
9. The course was one of the best I have had at this college.	1	2	3	4	5	X

YOUR FURTHER COMMENTS ARE INVITED:

_____

_____

_____

*Sample evaluations from Saldin (1984).

3

Student Advising

Rosemarie Bosler
Sharon L. Levin

❖ BASIC STUDENT ADVISING

When faculty members have the opportunity to interface with students outside of the classroom, the interaction has the potential to influence a student's success in college (Frost, 1997; Pascarella & Terensini, 1993) and affords students with a greater potential for growth and development. Meetings with the academic adviser are one of a student's most effective out-of-class relationships. Unfortunately, many faculty members are not comfortable serving as academic advisers for several reasons. According to the American College Testing Program (Levy, 1995), 98% of faculty members serve as academic advisers to students, most receive sparse preparation for this task in graduate school and are compelled to learn how to advise through extensive on-the-job experience. An increasing level of complexity exists as a result of increased curricular choices and the pluralistic nature of today's student body. Hence, faculty members are seeking more guidance on how to serve as effective advisers.

Academic advising has been defined as "a systematic process based on a close student-adviser relationship intended to aid students in achieving educational, career, and personal goals through the utilization of the full range of institutional and community resources" (Winston & Miller, 1991). This chapter takes a holistic approach to student advising that includes academic planning, career aspirations, and personal aspects of students' lives. Not only can the holistic approach benefit students, it can be rewarding to faculty members because it is an opportunity to contribute to students' success in a meaningful way.

It is assumed that advisers are well versed in explaining the college catalog and course scheduling booklet. Effective advising is much more than reiterating the information in campus publications, however. Some colleges and universities provide training for faculty serving as academic advisers. Unfortunately, those institutions that do provide training usually do so in a 1-day or half-day workshop format (Ryan, 1995), which is less than adequate for the complexity of issues faced by today's students. These training sessions usually focus on institutional policies and curricular requirements that provide the adviser with information regarding the college or university. Unfortunately, these training sessions fail to address adult human development theories and human relational skills necessary to handle the numerous issues students bring to advising sessions. An understanding of adult human development theories augments the administrative aspects of advising by making the adviser more aware and more sensitive to issues confronted in adulthood by students. In addition, students learn human relational skills by observing the adviser's behavior when interacting with other faculty members, administrators, and staff at the college or university.

Faculty members who want to read more about a conceptual model of effective advising should consider reading O'Banion's (1972) seminal article describing a developmental model of advising. This model identifies five steps that faculty should use for effective advising by encouraging their advisees to explore

1. Life goals
2. Vocational goals
3. Program choices
4. Course choices
5. Scheduling of courses

Given the lack of sufficient academic, institutional, and psychological training for faculty advisers, it is no surprise that advising is not a critical factor in the promotion and tenure process. Furthermore, the administrative aspects of advising sometimes come as an inconvenience to some faculty members, causing them to rank advising as a nonpriority. Effective academic advising is a fundamental element in student development and retention, however, making it essential to the total teaching process. This chapter provides guidelines for dealing with several major advising situations, including ethics, availability, working the system, and student growth. It also covers tips for handling administrative issues, career development, internships, and foreign students.

❖ ACADEMIC ISSUES

Administrative

Providing information concerning institutional policies and procedures minimizes student frustration and contributes to student success. When asked to identify the top three characteristics of a good adviser, students cited knowledge of institutional and curricular policies most often (see Appendix 3.1). Students should be advised of important dates in the academic calendar, such as

- course registration dates,
- drop-add dates,
- withdrawal dates, and
- graduation deadlines.

Students should be advised of important policies that may affect them, such as

- fees for late registration,
- tuition refund policies,
- unpaid fines and their effect on grades and graduation, and
- minimum credit requirements for maintaining financial aid.

Curricular Information

An understanding of all majors and minors offered at the institution is required for effective advising. Some students do not declare a major until the sophomore or junior year. These students should be encouraged to take a variety of classes in as many different disciplines as possible. This approach may enlighten the student to discover unknown interests and talents. Although many graduate students choose the degree program they are interested in before taking classes, some do not. In addition, after taking courses, some graduate students discover areas of study they had not previously chosen and may want to change their plan of study. The following checklist may be used to guide students toward declaring a major or minor.

The adviser should

- stress the importance of declaring a major or minor to graduate in a timely manner,
- encourage the student to reflect on the courses he or she has taken to identify interests,
- assist students in the process of choosing a major or minor by asking probing questions about their interests, skills, academic acumen, and career goals,
- encourage the student to declare a major before entering the junior year, and
- explain the administrative aspects of declaring a major or minor.

Seeking Academic Support

Most colleges and universities offer some form of academic services to enhance students' potential to earn good grades. The problem is that some students rarely seek help from these services unless prompted to do so. This is particularly true with foreign students from cultures where seeking help is discouraged and considered cheating. In these situations, the adviser should assure the advisee that student support services are designed to assist all students in achieving academic success and should therefore be used when appropriate.

As advisers, we have access to student records, which usually include SAT and GRE scores, transcripts, and entry exam scores. Because we have more information than any one professor would have about a particular student, we are in a unique position to assess students' strengths and weaknesses. It is incumbent on the adviser to stress the importance of using the academic support services on campus to increase students' study skills, writing abilities, and test scores.

The adviser should provide students with information on available academic student services, such as

- the writing center,
- the testing center, and
- the tutoring center.

Curricular Requirements

Most colleges and universities have requirements for all students expecting to graduate with a distinct degree. In addition, specific courses are usually required for major fields of study.

Advisers should encourage students to take courses that satisfy their major and core curricular requirements. It is usually advisable for students to take courses that satisfy requirements in every semester. The adviser should discourage students from trying to satisfy core requirements before beginning major requirements.

Advising for all students should include the following:

- Knowing the core requirements: Advisers should be well-informed about institutional curricular requirements in all majors because many students do not declare a major until later in their academic career, or they change their major.
- Knowing discipline variety requirements: Some colleges and universities require students to take courses from a variety of disciplines to ensure a well-rounded education. Advisers should keep accurate records to ensure that the advisee is meeting all discipline variety requirements.
- Knowing minimum credit requirement for graduation: Students should know that they must earn a minimum number of credits to graduate even if they have met all core and major and minor requirements.

Advising for specific majors and minors should include the following:

- Having an understanding of all program offerings in the institution. Sometimes advisees are assigned to an adviser who teaches in a discipline other than the student's interest. In these cases, advisers should have some understanding of the different major and minor requirements within the institution.
- Assisting the student in the identification and attainment of educational goals that will benefit the student upon graduation and subsequent entry into graduate school or the workforce.

Grievance Policies

Through the process of advising, a personal relationship develops between the student and adviser. In some ways, students view their adviser as a personal advocate. It is not uncommon for an advisee to view the adviser as the initial person to contact when he or she is troubled by any issue in his or her life, especially if the issue is related to experiences on campus. To minimize the stress students experience during their time on campus, the adviser should ensure that students follow proper protocol for filing a grievance. Encouraging students to follow a protocol for filing a grievance in college will serve as a model for them should they need to file a grievance in any aspect of their professional life.

Advisers should inform students of the process for filing a grievance about a professor, grade, or other academic issue. Although each institution has a different process to handle students' grievances, academic culture dictates that the first step in the grievance process is for the student to speak directly to the professor with whom he or she has a grievance. There are some exceptions, however, in the case of international students. Confronting a professor with a grievance might be almost impossible for many foreign students because of the high regard of a professor in a native culture. In these instances, the adviser will need to mediate.

It is not atypical for students to bypass this important first step in the grievance process and discuss a grievance with their adviser. It is the adviser's role to instruct the student to speak with his or her professor first. The adviser should not engage in dialogue with the advisee regarding any grievance until the student has spoken to his or her professor about the issue to avoid interfering with the student–professor relationship. It is the role of the adviser to be available for consultation if the student is unable to get satisfaction from his or her professor. Furthermore, if the nature of the grievance is such that the professor allegedly behaved unprofessionally or unethically, the adviser may want to be more involved as soon as he or she learns of the grievance. In cases that involve violation of the Civil Rights Act, the adviser's role should be to protect both the student and the institution.

❖ AVAILABILITY

To advise students in a timely manner, advisers must be available to students. Given the varied technological means of communication, faculty should provide students with multiple ways to reach them by supplying their telephone numbers, fax numbers, e-mail addresses, office location, and office hours. Using a preferred mode of communication gives the student a better chance of reaching the adviser and receiving a return communication in a timely manner. When asked to identify the top three characteristics of a good adviser, students identified availability as one of them (see Appendix 3.1).

❖ CAREER ISSUES

Many colleges and universities have career development programs on campus. Students should be advised of the services offered by these programs. In addition, students expect their adviser to have some knowledge of career possibilities in their field; these may not always match students' interests, however. In these cases, students can be directed to the career development programs, if available. Another avenue for career information is the Internet. Advisees should be encouraged to search the Internet for information concerning career options and job openings. A brief checklist that may be useful for career advising follows:

- Assist students in the identification of their career goals by asking probing questions. It is not necessary for students to be able to answer the questions on the spot. Students should be advised to write down questions, reflect on them, and return in a few weeks with their thoughts written down.

- Describe the various areas of practice related to the student's major. Some career options are obviously attached to certain majors; others are not as obvious. For example, a business major with an interest in art may want to open a gallery, manage a museum, or sell institutional art to large organizations. Advisers should encourage students to think broadly and not narrow their options by choosing the most typical career associated with their major.

- Identify career options that require graduate education and those that require only a baccalaureate degree. Not all students are financially or intellectually suitable for graduate school. Advisers should encourage each student to reach for his or her individual potential.

- Refer students to institutional resources where they can obtain information concerning career options, for example, a career development center.

❖ ETHICAL ISSUES

Although some aspects of advising use clearly delineated guidelines, other aspects do not. Ethical issues of advising are those that fall in the gray zone of decision making rather than obvious black or white situations. These ambiguous situations require advisers to consider carefully a multitude of variables in decision making. The nature of ethical issues results from uncertainty and a lack of precise guidelines to handle these issues; therefore, this section is not intended to prescribe specific guidance. Rather, it is intended to heighten your awareness of typical ethical issues that advisers face. Table 3.1 summarizes some ethical issues of advising and possible responses to consider.

❖ STUDENT GROWTH AND DEVELOPMENT ISSUES

In a recent study on advising, 99% of respondents agreed that academic advising aids personal development for students (Texas Higher Education Coordinating Board, 1995). Regardless of the age at which the student enters college or university, he or she will continue to develop

Table 3.1 Ethical Issues of Advising

Ethical Issues	Points to Consider	Possible Ways to Mitigate Ethical Issues
Confidentiality	• Student records • Parents' request for information • Other faculty and administrators' requests for information	• Detailed records of all meetings should be kept in a secured location. • Parents do NOT have the right to see student records—advise parents to speak with their child. • Do not discuss student records with anyone other than the student.
Relationship issues	• Professional relationship • Dual relationships	• Develop a professional advisor–advisee relationship—avoid close friendships. • If advisee is also a student in your class, maintain objectivity in grading.
Competence	• Accurate information • Special circumstances • Placing blame	• Offer accurate information to advisees; if you are unsure, seek accurate information before answering the student's question. • If you make special considerations for an advisee, put them in writing, give a copy to the advisee, and put a copy in the student's file. • Never blame another student, professor, or administrator—this further frustrates the advisee; just try to resolve the issue.
Counseling	• Professional help	• Advisors are not trained as psychologists. Refer advisees to professional resources when the student's problems are beyond academic advisement.

physically and psychologically during his or her academic career. Therefore, an understanding of adult human development theories such as those offered by Erikson (1959), Gilligan (1982), Hudson (1991), and Levinson (1978, 1986) should provide guidance when advising students.

It is probable that students will experience life-cycle events, both positive and negative, during their time in college. Although faculty members are neither expected nor encouraged to administer psychological therapy to advisees, an element of the adviser's role is to provide support for students facing personal and emotional problems.

Generally, the administration informs faculty about institutional services available for students. Most colleges and universities have counseling on campus available for students dealing with personal problems. Some students will be proactive about seeking help from campus counselors, whereas others will need encouragement to make their first appointment. Advisers may want to discuss the advisee's personal issues (without mentioning the student's name) with a campus counselor to get advice on how to encourage the student to seek psychological help. Colleges and universities that do not provide on-campus counseling services should offer a referral service so students can seek affordable counseling in the community. At a minimum, advisers should provide students with information on personal services available for their use, such as

- psychological counseling,
- health care center, and
- services for students with physical limitations.

❖ INTERNSHIPS

Andragogy (Knowles, 1973) looks at the art and science of helping adults learn. One way to help adults learn is to provide an opportunity for them to learn using the method that best suits them. Research shows that adult learners absorb 10% of what they read, 20% of what they hear, 30% of what they read and hear, 50% of what they hear and see, 70% of what they say, and 90% of what they do by themselves with others. Adult learners learn best by *doing*, and therefore the internship experience is one of the greatest opportunities for students' growth and development. The internship experience can be an opportunity for students to learn the skills necessary to succeed in their future professional lives.

The internship experience is a triad relationship among the student, the faculty adviser, and the employing supervisor. All three parties have responsibilities for the student to complete the internship successfully. In some instances, the internship is a student's first employment experience. In this case, he or she will need more guidance, especially to obtain the internship position. The adviser's role is to provide guidance to the intern in the following areas:

- Develop a resume. Refer the student to the career development office of the college or university. If a career development office does not exist, suggest that students seek help from the following resources:

1. Most word processing programs have resume templates that guide the development of a resume. For example, in Microsoft Word, students can easily produce resumes by choosing from different styles available on existing templates.
2. Many other methods of assisting in the writing of resumes are available in book form and computer programs. The student can consult a favorite local bookstore or computer software outlet.

- Suggest that students participate in role-playing interview sessions with their colleagues. It is helpful to provide students with a list of commonly asked interview questions. Appendix 3.2 includes a list of possible questions asked at an internship interview.

- After the interview, suggest that students write thank you letters to all interviewers.

- Once students have attained employment, a formalized agreement between the employer and the college or university should be signed by the parties in the triad relationship: the intern, the employing supervisor, and the academic supervisor. Most colleges and universities have internship agreement documents to formalize this process. For those that do not, a sample internship agreement can be found in Appendix 3.3.

- The adviser's role with the intern shifts after employment begins; the focus is to encourage interns to develop skills in the workplace associated with high performance. Advisers should stress the importance of attendance, punctuality, and accountability.

- Another function served by advisers is that of having some contact with the employment supervisor. The degree of interaction between the academic adviser and the employment supervisor will vary depending on institutional requirements, discipline-related factors, the maturity and experience of the intern, and the employing supervisor. At a minimum, the adviser should speak with the employing supervisor at the beginning of the internship to clarify the learning objectives identified by the student and the adviser. The adviser should inform the employing supervisor that he or she is available for consultation throughout the internship, if necessary.

• During the internship period, advisers should encourage advisees to have a positive attitude while serving the employing agency as self-reliant workers. Suggest that they see the internship as an opportunity to apply the theories they learned in the classroom, to develop skills useful in the workplace, and to network for potential employment opportunities. A successful internship may result in a letter of reference or a job offer for the intern.

• A professional relationship between the college or university and the organization providing the internship may result in future internship opportunities for other students, collaboration on program or curricular development to enhance the connection between what is taught in college and what is needed in the workplace, or contacts for mentoring programs or shadowing experiences for other students.

❖ TROUBLESHOOTING: MAKING THE
   SYSTEM WORK FOR STUDENTS

In some respects, all student advising can be considered troubleshoot-ing—or, to phrase it in a more positive light, minimizing the amount of difficulties the student faces while enrolled in the college or university. Faculty advisers are often viewed as advocates for advisees. This may require some of the following extraordinary efforts on the part of the adviser:

• Some students, especially those who are learning impaired or struggling with the language, may require special testing conditions. The student should be advised to request special testing conditions from the professor. If the professor is unwilling to accommodate the student's needs, then the adviser may intervene by speaking with the professor and explaining the student's special circumstances. It is advisable to seek the advice of the on-campus disabilities office, which is required to exist on every campus.

• Internship opportunities do not always coincide with the academic year. If a student has an opportunity for an internship that is a good learning experience but the drop-add period is over, then the adviser might allow the student to perform the internship in one semester and sign up for it in the following semester. It is important to make sure that the student officially registers for and pays for the internship credits. Otherwise, the transcript will not reflect that the class was taken.

- Sometimes students need assistance gaining access to administrators, staff, and other professors for various reasons. Given the personal relationships developed in the academic community, advisers may be able to communicate a student's needs in a way that a colleague is more sympathetic to.

- If a student is preparing to graduate and realizes that he or she is lacking 1 or 2 credits, the adviser may create a 1-credit-elective independent study project that allows the student to graduate as planned.

There is a fine line between making the system work for the student and jeopardizing the integrity of the system for the institution. As professionals, we can assess the degree to which we are willing to go to bat for our students. Obviously, it is not in the best interest of the student or the institution if advisers bend the rules too far to meet student needs.

❖ ADVISING FOREIGN STUDENTS

Today's foreign students attending colleges or universities in the United States are characterized as traditional age, many from developing countries, who intend to return to their home country at the end of their educational program. This does not negate the presence of other students on American campuses; it contributes to the diversity of the population. These students often have language difficulties, lack cultural understanding, and experience culture shock, financial and legal issues, and difficulty selecting relevant academic programs (Millett-Sorensen & Crownhart, 1985). Selection of faculty advisers capable of working with this special population needs to be done thoughtfully and not randomly. Current and former foreign student advisers identified characteristics, gleaned from their personal experiences, necessary for these advisers. The three most important personal qualities for foreign student advisers to possess are cross-cultural sensitivity, personal warmth, and willingness to help and be patient (Millett-Sorensen & Crownhart, 1985). The three most critical skills such advisers need are cross-cultural counseling, public relations, and cross-cultural communication.

In many large academic institutions, foreign student advising is done by professionals, nonfaculty members trained specifically in foreign student advising. Many institutions do not provide this specialized service, however. Smaller institutions or those with smaller numbers of foreign students usually "add on" foreign student advisees to the regular advising load of faculty members. This portion of the chapter is written for faculty members charged with advising foreign students.

Inculturation in this case into the academic scene is done, then, by the department advisers. Internal support may be found from other student service offices found across colleges and universities such as financial aid, career counseling, the learning center, and residence directors. External support may be sought from organizations such as the National Association of Foreign Student Affairs (NAFSA), located in Washington, DC. An important text for foreign student advisers is the *Advisor's Manual for Federal Regulations Affecting Foreign Students and Scholars* (Cotten, 1998).

As noted earlier in this chapter, the role of faculty adviser is critical to the academic success of the student (Frost, 1997; Pascarella & Terensini, 1993). The first responsibility of the foreign student adviser is managerial; this is very much the same for any advisee across institutions. Advising goes beyond the managerial aspects of identifying courses and signing registration forms. Advisers motivate and encourage students, help students meet institutional requirements in a timely manner, provide guidelines for using advising time efficiently and effectively, designate regular "drop-in" office hours for short informal discussions, initiate and return phone calls, assume the role of advocate, explain aspects of college life, maintain an academic portfolio, and move students from dependence to independence. Appendixes 3.4 and 3.5 cite managerial ideas for advising sessions, not only focusing on the interaction between the advisee and adviser but covering many managerial tasks at the same time. Whatever it takes to make advising sessions more efficient should be used. This enables the advisee and adviser to interact on more in-depth issues specifically relevant to the student.

Language Problems

Problems with language are generally handled "in house," that is, the college or university usually provides the help foreign students need in this area. Difficulties might include inadequate knowledge of English, lack of practice listening to a native speaker, inability to comprehend innuendoes of the language, and misunderstanding the jargon of specific academic disciplines. Several options and combinations therefore will prove beneficial. The most likely solution for a student experiencing a great deal of difficulty is to make sure the student is enrolled in an English as a second language course. Many other difficulties will be eliminated once the student has had enough practice "living" with the language. Some interventions will help the advisee through some difficult times, however. One common criticism of foreign students is that they are unable to follow their professors during lecture and demonstration classes, thus diminishing their ability to succeed. The adviser might suggest the following:

- Have students tape lectures, with the instructor's permission. This will free the student from trying to listen and take notes simultaneously. The student can concentrate on listening to the instructor during class and then listen to the tape for further reinforcement and note taking.
- Encourage students to form a study or support group.
- Assist students in finding an appropriate tutor.
- Encourage professors to sponsor problem sessions.
- Encourage students to find alternative texts.

It would save a great deal of time if foreign student advisers could pull this information together and have a small pamphlet ready for the students at the beginning of the year.

Cultural Difficulties

The second major problem a foreign advisee might experience is culture shock. This brings us to another responsibility of the faculty adviser—successfully moving the advisee through the process of inculturation. This depends on the personal qualities and skills of the faculty adviser. Foreign student advisers must be prepared to explain U.S. culture and values to the advisee, understand students' academic preparation, ensure that the course of studies pursued will be beneficial when the student returns to his or her own country, and identify support or community groups the advisee might like to join. Advisers should prepare students to return home (Millett-Sorensen & Crownhart, 1985).

One advantage of going abroad to study is one's immersion into another culture. Faculty in general and advisers specifically go out of their way to provide positive cultural experiences for their foreign students. There is an assumption that the student will return to his or her own country with a better appreciation and understanding of American culture, as well as with professional or career know-how. It is just as important and advantageous for the adviser to study the advisee's culture and values beyond stereotypical misrepresentation. One excellent resource for general information on various cultures is *Communicating with Strangers: An Approach to Intercultural Communication* (GudyKunst & YunKim, 1992). These authors examine cross-cultural understanding and communication. They identify valued-based cultural variables that provide an excellent knowledge base for faculty advisers. When there is little or no understanding of cultural differences, breakdown in the communication process results and academic success is jeopardized.

One section of *Communicating with Strangers* (GudyKunst & YunKim, 1992) stands out as being clear on the variables that influence cultural thought and behavior and can ultimately have a bearing on foreign student success. Some of the variables include how the society views individuals versus collective communication, power, and time orientation. Table 3.2 summarizes a few of the variables concerning cross-cultural communication as identified by several studies and should be considered when advising foreign students (Hofstede, 1991, 1993).

Most Likert-type scales, like cultural forms, tend to cluster each society at one end of the scale. There is variation in the distribution, but society as a whole has a tendency to cluster toward one end or the other. Successful advisers are aware of the cultural characteristics of specific groups and how those characteristics influence advising needs. It is highly recommended that advisers read books with a focus on cross-cultural communication (GudyKunst & YunKim, 1992; Hofstede, 1991, 1993).

Financial and Legal Issues

One topic GudyKunst and YunKim (1992) tend to avoid is that of financial aid. That is best left to the financial aid officer(s). There might

Table 3.2 Cross-Cultural Variables

Power Distance	
Large	*Small*
Instructor-student relationship inequality	Instructor-student relationship is basically equal
Examples: France, Hong Kong, Indonesia, West Africa, China	United States, Germany, The Netherlands

Individualism	
Individualist Societies	*Collectivist Societies*
Individual participation is desired Individual goals take precedence over group goals Conflict is welcome Competition is expected Examples: United States, Germany, The Netherlands, France	Limited individual-initiated participation Group goals are more important than individual goals Conflict is avoided Collaboration is expected China, Hong Kong, Indonesia, West Africa

Uncertainty Avoidance	
Strong	*Weak*
Expects professors to be experts Favors structured learning situations Expects reward for accuracy Examples: France, Japan, Russia	Respects a professor who says "I do not know" Dislikes structure Expects reward for originality United States, Hong Kong, Indonesia

Masculinity/Femininity	
High Masculinity	*High Femininity*
High student visibility Openly competitive Ambitious, with a focus on career opportunities Failure to perform is disastrous Examples: United States, Japan, Hong Kong, Germany	Student is less visible and eager Goal of solidarity Nurturing, with a focus on intrinsic interest in subject Failure to perform well is not a serious problem The Netherlands

Time Orientation	
Long-Term	*Short-Term*
Values tradition Examples: China, Hong Kong, Japan	Change is highly valued United States, France, West Africa, Indonesia

SOURCE: Hofstede (1991, 1993).

be times when the foreign advisee does not understand some issues related to his or her financial benefits or responsibilities, however, and for any number of reasons might ask for the adviser's help. At this point, the adviser may choose to become a mediator, not by finding the answer for the student but by assisting the student to find the correct information. Financial aid issues usually require a joint meeting with person(s) from the financial aid office or the treasurer of the college or university.

Advisers frequently encounter a foreign student from a developing country who had someone from his or her home country sponsor the student's study in America. To be admitted to a college or university, students usually need to be able to pay in full the first semester or full year's tuition and residence expenses. Once students are here and they successfully complete the first semester or year, the foreign funding stops. It is important to recognize that this might happen to an advisee, and the adviser needs to be prepared to advise students as to where they might find necessary funds to complete their education.

The same avoidance tactic is true for legal issues; refer students to the experts on campus. We recommend the *Adviser's Manual for Federal Regulations Affecting Foreign Students and Scholars* (Yenkin, 1994) for advising students on legal issues.

❖ ADVISING STUDENTS WITH DISABILITIES

The Americans with Disabilities Act (ADA) of 1990 does not replace Section 504 of the Rehabilitation Act of 1973. It is more comprehensive and is of special interest to educational institutions, both public and private, because they must be in compliance regardless of federal funding (Kalivoda & Higbee, 1994; Lissner, 1997). Section 504 of the Rehabilitation Act of 1973 states, "No otherwise qualified handicapped individual in the United States shall, solely by reason of his handicap, be excluded from participation in, be denied the benefits of, or be subject to discrimination under any program receiving federal financial assistance."

The ADA states, "The nation's proper goals regarding individuals with disabilities are to assure equality of opportunity, full participation, independent living, and economic self-sufficiency for persons with disabilities."

Title II of the ADA addresses issues pertaining to public and private educational institutions. To be in compliance with these acts (Lissner, 1997), colleges and universities are required to

- have handicap accessibility,
- make reasonable accommodations,
- provide notices of nondiscrimination,
- make academic adjustments,
- provide equal opportunities,
- provide personal, academic, and career counseling, and
- safeguard confidentiality.

No particular policy or set of guidelines can anticipate all the situations that might arise in the effort to implement or comply with the law. The Civil Rights Division, Office on the Americans with Disabilities Act, U.S. Department of Justice provides on-line experts to answer questions any institution might have. This assistance is available Monday through Friday by calling (202) 514-0301 (voice) or (202) 514-0383 (TTY).

Most institutions have designated offices to handle all matters regarding the ADA and the Rehabilitation Act. Advisers need to know institutional policies because there will be times when students with disabilities are assigned to them, so advisers often become advocates for these students. Very often, students with nonobvious disabilities such as attention deficit disorder or learning disabilities do not self-identify when they are making application to an institution. They often confide in their academic advisers once the semester gets under way and they begin to experience academic problems, however. Advisers need to encourage students to self-identify with the compliance officer on campus. Institutions are not required to make accommodations for students without proper documentation of the disability. The adviser should inform students of their rights and encourage them to get the proper documentation so the process of accommodation can begin.

It is not the adviser's responsibility to make known a student's disability to the student's professors.

❖ ADVISING THESIS AND DISSERTATION STUDENTS

Many students come to graduate school directly from a bachelor's program; others have had full careers and are looking for opportunities to change that career; and still others come specifically for professional advancement. Regardless of why or how they came, students must meet certain benchmarks along the way. The final benchmark for the master's degree candidate is the thesis; for the doctoral candidate it is the dissertation; and for some, one leads to the other. The thesis or dissertation adviser's challenge is to find the best way to move the student to the conclusion of his or her program, which means getting students to research, write, and defend their final products. We discuss thesis advising and dissertation advising together because the process is similar, even though the product differs. The main distinction between the two is that the thesis expands on existing research, whereas originality is expected in the dissertation.

Though each college and university has different requirements and terminology differs, there are certain standard steps in developing the thesis and dissertation.

- Identify and refine a topic.
- Select a thesis or dissertation adviser or director and committee.
- Develop a working bibliography.
- Prepare and defend a proposal.
- Collect data.
- Prepare final document.
- Prepare for defense.

Long, Convey, and Chwalek (1985) have written a book on getting the dissertation completed; it is recommended for students involved in research. These authors identify obstacles and recommend possible solutions; they take the reader systematically through the process mentioned above. Some issues are not included in Long et al., however: what to look for in a thesis or dissertation adviser, the advisee's personal style of learning and working, and personal satisfaction.

Thesis/Dissertation Adviser

In many cases, the student's academic adviser might not be the adviser guiding the student through the thesis or dissertation. Care must be taken to help the student select this special adviser; often the academic adviser can be very helpful in guiding the student with this decision because the adviser has had the opportunity to work with the student over several semesters and is knowledgeable about how the student operates. Several models of advising have been identified over the last decade, yet one stands above the others for advising students doing a thesis or a dissertation: mentoring. According to Anderson and Shannon (1988), mentoring is an intentional, insightful, and supportive process "in which a more skilled or more experienced person, serving as a role model, nurtures, befriends, teaches, sponsors, encourages and counsels a less skilled or less experienced person for the purpose of promoting the latter's profession and personal development" (p. 39). This can be a very rewarding experience for both the adviser and the advisee if there is a good match between the student and her or his topic and the experience and research of the adviser.

Personal Style of Learning and Working

In recent years, educators at all levels have been inundated with various theories of learning style. To name just a few, there is Gardner's (1983) multiple intelligence research on right brain and left brain, top-down or bottom-up, learning and Hermann's (1988) four quadrants of learning. All styles of learning are equally valid. Educators try to teach to all styles to help students feel comfortable operating in all modes. When students feel stressed, however, they tend to move toward their most comfortable learning style. The theory of top-down, bottom-up learning might be helpful for the adviser to gain insight into the learner and therefore be able to direct the advisee effectively. Top-down learners like to gain an overall perspective of the subject; bottom-up learners like to have a solid foundation of the subject before they proceed to information that is more general. Top-down learners are known as *groupers*, bottom-up learners are known as *stringers*. Table 3.3 provides a brief description of the two types.

Table 3.3 Groupers Versus Stringers

Groupers	Stringers

Take a broad view of any subject
Search out general principles
Relate topic to as many other areas of
  knowledge as possible
Quick to find relationships
Draw parallels among different areas of study
	Take a systematic, methodical approach
	Establish a list of clearly defined goals
	Consider facts related directly to the topic
	  under study
	Ignore less relevant material

SOURCE: Gross (1991).

Much schooling has favored the stringers approach to learning; this can prove to be an obstacle to the groupers, especially in major research projects such as the thesis or dissertation. Gross (1991) offers suggestions for working with groupers' styles. This information will be beneficial at the choice of topic phase of the thesis or dissertation.

Personal Satisfaction

One goal of the graduate adviser and advisee is personal satisfaction. There is a certain mutuality about this satisfaction. The adviser has completed her or his responsibility to challenge, guide, direct, and encourage an advisee during an intense period of academic work. In turn, through the completion of the thesis or dissertation, the advisee is validated, not only by the adviser but also by the institution, as a scholar. This is personal satisfaction for most.

❖ CONCLUSION

Being an adviser requires many of the same skills used for classroom management. Often, professors are confronted with unique and challenging issues in the classroom that require impromptu responses. The interpersonal skills used for effective teaching are also useful for advising sessions. Knowledge of the topic, willingness to listen to students' concerns, and eagerness to help students find answers to their questions create a good student-adviser relationship.

In the classroom environment, we teach students how to use and manipulate the information we give them in different ways. Although it may appear that all the input is from the professor—especially in the beginning—as the student becomes more independent, he or she should be encouraged to develop into a self-directed learner.

Likewise, the goal of the academic adviser is to move the advisee from dependence to independence. During the beginning of the student's academic career, she or he will need to learn institutional rules, policies, and culture. Academic advisers can alleviate an advisee's stress by empowering him or her to be self-directed. Although the role of the academic adviser cannot be overemphasized, the ultimate goal of the adviser is to become nonessential by the end of the advisee's academic career.

❖ REFERENCES

Anderson, E., & Shannon, A. (1988). Toward a conceptualization of mentoring. *Journal of Teacher Education, 39*(1), 38-42.

Cotten, C. (1998). *Advisor's Manual for Federal Regulations Affecting Foreign Students and Scholars.* Washington, DC: NAFSA.

Erikson, E. H. (1959). *Identity and the life cycle.* New York: International Universities Press.

Frost, S. R. (1997). *Academic advising for student success: A system of shared responsibility* (ASHE-ERIC Higher Education Report). Washington, DC: Association for the Study of Higher Education.

Gardner, H. (1983). *Frames of mind: The theory of multiple intelligences.* New York: Basic Books.

Gilligan, C. (1982). *In a different voice: Psychological theory and women's development.* Cambridge, MA: Harvard University Press.

Gross, R. (1991). *Peak learning: A master course in learning how to learn.* New York: Tarcher Teriger.

GudyKunst, W., & YunKim, Y. (1992). *Communicating with strangers.* New York: McGraw-Hill.

Hermann, N. (1988). *The creative brain.* Lake Lure, NC: Brain Books.

Hofstede, G. (1991). *Cultures and organizations: Software of the mind.* New York: McGraw-Hill.

Hofstede, G. (1993). Cultural constraint in management theories. *Academy of Management Executive, 7*(1), 81-94.

Hudson, F. M. (1991). *The adult years: Mastering the art of self-renewal.* San Francisco: Jossey-Bass.

Kalivoda, K., & Higbee, J. (1994). Implementing the Americans with Disabilities Act: Questions and answers. *Journal of Humanistic Education and Development, 32*(3), 133-137.

Knowles, M. (1973). *The adult learner: A neglected species.* Houston: Gulf.

Levinson, D. J. (1978). *The seasons of a man's life.* New York: Knopf.

Levinson, D. J. (1986). A conception of adult development. *American Psychologist, 41*(1), 3-13.

Levy, N. (1995). *American College Testing 16th Edition.* Indianapolis: MacMillan Publishing Company.

Lissner, L. S. (1997, March). *Policy elements in the ADA & Section 504.* Paper presented at ACPA/NASPA conference, Chicago.

Long, T., Convey, J., & Chwalek, A. (1985). *Completing dissertations in the behavioral sciences and education.* San Francisco: Jossey-Bass.

Millett-Sorensen, K., & Crownhart, S. (1985, May). *Foreign student advising as a profession: The 1984 survey.* Paper presented at the Annual National Association for Foreign Student Affairs Conference, Long Beach, CA.

O'Banion, T. (1972). Academic advising in two-year colleges: A national survey. *Journal of College Student Personnel, 5*(4), 411-419.

Pascarella, E., & Terensini, P. (1993). *How college affects students.* San Francisco: Jossey Bass.

Ryan, C. (1995). Professional development and training for faculty advisers. *New Directions for Teaching and Learning, 62,* 35-42.

Texas Higher Education Coordinating Board. (1995). *Report on academic advising.* Austin: TASP Office Universities Division.

Winston, R. B., & Miller, R. K. (Eds.). (1991). *Administration and leadership in student affairs.* Muncie IN: Actualizing Student Development.

Yenkin, A. (1994). *Adviser's manual for federal regulations affecting foreign students and scholars.* Cranberry Township, PA: NAFSA.

Appendix 3.1

Good Adviser Characteristics

We surveyed undergraduate and graduate students in the spring 1997 semester and asked them to identify the top characteristics of an adviser. Their responses in order of frequency cited:

A good adviser is

1. knowledgeable of institutional policies and curricular requirements,
2. a good listener and easy to talk to,
3. available and easy to get in touch with,
4. people oriented and has a sense of humor, and
5. caring, patient, willing to help, and shows concern for the student.

Appendix 3.2

Interview Questions

Frequently asked questions for internship interviewees:

- Why do you want to be an intern here?
- Describe your educational background.
- What specific knowledge and skills do you bring to this work environment?
- What career do you plan to seek after graduation?
- Why should I give you this internship?

Encourage the student to do some research on the company before going to the interview. This will enable the student to ask intelligent questions about the company and assess whether the internship opportunity is best suited to his or her career goals. In addition, researching potential internship opportunities before the interview will serve as a model for the student when he or she is interviewing for future employment opportunities.

Appendix 3.3

Sample Internship Agreement

Student Information

Student Name: _____

Phone Numbers: Day: _____ Night: _____ Fax: _____

E-mail Address: _____

Declared Major: _____

Academic Adviser: _____

Course Information

Course Number: _____ Credits: _____ Hours per Week: _____

Semester of Internship: _____ Faculty Supervisor: _____

Internship Information

Internship Agency: _____

Agency Address: _____

Agency Phone Numbers: _____ Fax: _____

Employment Supervisor, Name, and Title: _____

_____

Objectives of Internship

On a separate piece of paper, list the measurable performance goals and objectives for this internship; you may attach a job description. Include a reading list, the planned midterm evaluation, the planned final evaluation report, and the format of the daily journal you will keep during the internship.

Signatures

Student: _____

Faculty Supervisor: _____

Employment Supervisor: _____

Appendix 3.4

The First Advising Session With a Foreign Student

Time: Approximately 45 to 60 minutes

Ask open-ended questions to learn more about your advisee.
- What brought you to this college?
- What do you think will be your greatest challenge over the next few years?
- What is your greatest achievement?
- What are you hoping to do after you graduate?

Share some of your own personal experiences.
- Length of time at the university or college
- Areas of academic and personal interest
- Other information pertinent to the situation and/or advisee

Briefly explain the academic program (remember that these students have been through orientation and are probably on overload).

Briefly explain current semester course offerings.

Register the student for the semester (do not plan the total degree program at this time; get the student settled into the semester).

Make an appointment to meet within the next 2 or 3 weeks (the purpose of this subsequent meeting is to see how everything is going, identify any problem(s), and target necessary support services the student may need).

Encourage students to take responsibility to plan for a formal academic advising session. This provides ample time for deeper conversations essential to ongoing professional development.

Appendix 3.5

Preparation for Conference to Schedule Classes

- Read registration material carefully.
- Check to see what general and major requirements you have fulfilled.
- Identify courses you want to take (rule of thumb: Select some courses from your major and some from institutional requirements).
- Check to see if there are any prerequisites.
- Check to see if there are conflicts.
- Make choices.

The following grid can help advisees think through their course scheduling before the advising session. Foreign students and students new to the academic community may need more help in sketching out a tentative schedule. Nevertheless, it is important to encourage all advisees to fill in the grid on their own to develop independence in the scheduling process as soon as possible.

Time/Day	Monday	Tuesday	Wednesday	Thursday	Friday	Saturday
8:00-9:00 am						
9:00-10:00	BIO 101, 9-9:50		BIO 101, 9-9:50		BIO 101, 9-9:50	
10:00-11:00	SPA 100, 10-10:50	MGT 200, 10-11:15	SPA 100, 10-10:50	MGT 200, 10-11:15	SPA 100, 10-10:50	
11:00-12:00						
12:00-1:00 pm	PHI 103, 12-12:50		PHI 103, 12-12:50		PHI 103, 12-12:50	
1:00-2:00						
2:00-3:00		SOC 100, 2-3:15		SOC 100, 2-3:15	BIO LAB, 2-5	
3:00-4:00						
4:00-5:00						
5:00-6:00						

4

Academic Research

Sharon Ahern Fechter

Every faculty member at virtually every 4-year college or university ultimately considers the question of research. There is really no mystery to research and publishing, yet somehow we have created a climate of apprehension when it comes to this aspect of our profession. What kind of research to engage in, which avenues to explore to disseminate that research, and how to go about getting the research published can be daunting considerations for untenured faculty members and are not to be dismissed by mid- and late-career academicians either.

Why is there such a focus on research, even at the so-called teaching institutions? The fact is that graduate education in the United States is among the strongest in the world, owing, in part, to the strong integration of research and teaching as well as the emphasis on research training. Although this reality came to be in the 20th century, it is clearly documented in the literature and well recognized among observers of higher education worldwide. Between the world wars, the emphasis on research was encouraged by private agencies (e.g., foundations) that made funds available for research. This was further fueled following World War II when public sources of funding, especially for science and technology, became available, giving rise to the tremendous growth of uni-

97

versity departments with a primary focus on research. (For a detailed discussion of the growth and development of the focus on research at institutions of higher learning, refer to Clark, 1995.) This focus on research, for better or worse, has pervaded higher education in the United States at virtually every level. Although research expectations can and do vary in scope and intensity from institution to institution, they become a consideration for faculty at the vast majority of colleges and universities in the United States.

❖ REASONS TO RESEARCH

As an individual faculty member, you research and seek to publish that research for a variety of reasons. A given is the overarching motivation to expand the body of knowledge and thereby move human civilization forward. In addition, giving back to one's discipline as well as to society at large constitutes a very real motivation and can become the dominant factor in the later stages of one's career. Furthermore, active involvement in and inquiry into the intellectual developments in a discipline contribute to effectiveness as a teacher. Finally, faculty members have traditionally been concerned with research as it relates to the process of tenure and promotion.

Other motivations to publish vary from individual to individual, and these are likely to undergo a number of transformations as you progress through your career. Shifting personal goals and interests and the fit or disconnect of these with institutional priorities shape the course of research as well. Defining and understanding your own academic passion not only will help you identify the course and content of your research, but will probably ultimately define the quality of that research.

❖ ON THE PATH TO PROMOTION AND TENURE

Although the definition of "appropriate research" for purposes of promotion and tenure varies from discipline to discipline, most institutions place a high value on the level of recognition among peers and the significance to the particular discipline of a given activity. Scholarly activity is typically demonstrated by evidence of sustained inquiry in an area of a discipline encompassing, but not limited to, publications or, as appropriate, artistic works and performances; receiving research grants and participating in funded research projects; and presentation of research findings at professional meetings.

Publications can take many shapes and forms, from the ever-present and possibly one of the most highly valued if not overrated article in a refereed journal to the introductory textbook to the snapshot insight of a newsletter article to the instant on-line communiqué of the latest research finding. Books, edited books, textbooks, and annotated bibliographies may all represent dedication and sustained scholarly inquiry, but each is likely to be valued differently in considerations about promotion and tenure. In some instances, academics may choose to publish research or insights on their own (and at their own expense) in a vanity press. Although such a publication might address the need to disseminate information and could, in fact, meet a need in the general public, publishing with a vanity press is unlikely to further your case for purposes of promotion and tenure. Choosing your research and publication venue is an important process, and understanding the benefits and drawbacks of each possibility for scholarship is critical as you establish your research agenda.

Although smaller colleges and comprehensive universities might value scholarship and professional activity as a unit, other institutions distinguish research and publication from service to the profession, with the expectation that faculty members have an additional obligation to maintain a high level of professional competence and to remain current in their field. Such institutional expectations motivate faculty members to support and assume an active role in appropriate professional organizations. Service activities in support of the profession are likely to include the following:

- Appointment in a scholarly capacity to a regional, state, or national position in a professional organization (e.g., service on committees or editorial boards)
- Holding a leadership or executive position in a professional organization
- General participation in professional organizations (e.g., attendance at annual meetings)
- Presenting papers at professional conferences
- Service in your professional discipline as a consultant
- Reviews of others' creative or scholarly work

You will probably be asked to provide evidence of your service to the profession. The demonstration of your service could include, but would not necessarily be limited to, the following types of evidence:

- Documented self-report of activities (e.g., conference programs, agendas, acknowledgments from colleagues, officers, committee chairs in your professional organizations)
- Written evaluations or statements of professional colleagues
- Published citations or acknowledgments of contributions in proceedings

Teaching and college- or university-related service activities are explored in other chapters.

As you progress through the years, it is a good idea to maintain a file of independent documentation of all professional activity. Promotion and tenure committees are unlikely to take into consideration self-reporting of professional activity that is not adequately documented.

❖ ESTABLISHING A RESEARCH AGENDA

A crucial first step in establishing a research agenda is to define clearly your purposes for researching and for publishing that research. These will undoubtedly change as you progress through your career or even as you move from institution to institution. If this kind of mobility is in the cards for you, establish your agenda accordingly.

In fact, it might be wise to focus on the portability of your research in any case. Faculty have noticed a growing and troublesome (for some) trend among some departments and institutions to place faculty on contract lines instead of on tenure lines. One faculty member in this situation at a large private research institution notes that the fact that she will never be afforded the opportunity to stand for tenure is problematic: "It raises many interesting questions regarding my status in the school and my feelings about my job." It also affects her research agenda and her level of willingness to participate in administrative activities— efforts that could be of less value should she seek a tenure-track slot at another institution and that rob valuable time and energy from pursuing her research. This faculty member's advice to new faculty is to tell them to organize their activities so that they are never trapped. That means that they should publish consistently in quality publications, that they can produce good to average student reviews, and, if working with doc students, they move them through at a regular pace.

> We are bogged down with administrative duties. It is a very big trap that new faculty get caught in (particularly because senior faculty, who don't want to administer, give the new people the tasks). My recommendation is that you will need to do some administration, but it should never overshadow the teaching or publishing activities. No faculty member at _____ will ever be promoted or tenured without a solid publication record. While teaching is talked about, it alone will not carry a decision.

On the same issue, Whicker, Kronenfield, and Strickland (1993) advise,

> Do not try to run the university or your department until you have tenure. . . . Your first priority should be to your own research and teaching, preferably performing service activities that are related to your own unique expertise. For those tenure candidates with ambitions of a career in university administration, much time remains after the tenure is approved to run the department, college, and university." (pp. 141-142).

Another consideration is the scope and intensity of your research. If your research is intimately linked with the very specific mission of a particular institution or within a very narrow specialization within a specific field (the scalpel model—see Whicker et al., 1993, pp. 76 ff.), you may be limiting your future career moves: "Develop a marketable record. . . . The best strategy . . . is to develop a record of professional productivity that would be appreciated and tenurable at a wide array of institutions, not just your own current institution" (p. 143).

Research and personal passions ideally go hand in hand, and it is a happy circumstance when these coincide with the agenda, both overt and implicit, of your institution. That is frequently not the case, however. So adjust the fit as best you can. If you are a first-year faculty member whose primary motivation is to be granted tenure, make sure that you fully understand the research expectations, both within your department and within the institution. Talk to current and former members of promotion and tenure committees and review recent successful cases.

In periodically reviewing the requirements with your department chair or academic dean, you may find that tenure committee members' assessments differ from those of administrators, particularly new administrators who are trying to forge new paths. If an administrator tells you that publishing on the Web, for example, is exactly the kind of innovative scholarship the department needs, yet members of the tenure committee clearly regard this with skepticism, you may want to be sure you include more traditional research venues in your agenda. In some institutions, administrators come and go with some frequency, and tenure committees may be more stable and less likely to change. In any case, it is a good idea to seek a mentor on the senior faculty (preferably one who is sufficiently self-assured not to be paranoid about your stealing her or his intellectual insights) to help guide your research agenda and to help you navigate the political waters.

Make an effort to understand the nature and mission of your institution. If you are at a large research university, accept the fact that you will be expected to publish books and numerous scholarly articles in first- and second-tier refereed journals, that single authorship (in many disciplines) may be preferable to joint authorship, and that, in the final analysis, publications will probably weigh more heavily than either teaching or service. One faculty member in a humanities discipline at a large research university notes that her chances of getting promoted are zero without a book.

On the other hand, many institutions define themselves primarily as teaching institutions, where research expectations are (theoretically!) reduced. Although such a vision may expand the avenues of publication you are open to pursue, don't be lulled into a false sense of security. Many faculty contend that a public posture focusing on excellence in teaching is confusing at best and little more than lip service at worst. Even in instances where there is a stated focus on teaching and current administrative support for this posture, the minimum expectation for promotion and tenure may ultimately include publications. One untenured faculty member at a small teaching institution expressed concern that a change in leadership could "change the rules" and thereby negatively affect her chances of getting tenure. A faculty member at a small comprehensive university notes that although there is a stated focus on excellence in teaching for promotion and tenure, "it is a necessary but not sufficient condition for either."

With fewer and fewer tenure slots available as colleges and universities shift to short- and long-term contracts, the competition is increasing for these tenure-track positions. The quality and quantity of your research may tip the scales in your favor.

The literature suggests, in fact, that research expectations are increasing everywhere and that longevity of quality service in the classroom and at the institution in general is, in and of itself, unlikely to result in the granting of tenure. What teaching institutions may afford, however, is the opportunity to have research that closely links teaching to scholarship be more highly valued in the tenure and promotion process. An untenured faculty member from a teaching institution notes that although some publication is necessary, "the order of preference is teaching, service, and then research," and textbooks and materials development are valued as part of the research expectation.

Quality materials development in the form of textbooks or survey texts that incorporate current disciplinary advances with innovative teaching techniques could, in this scenario, count as much or more than journal articles. Research and scholarly activity that focus on pedagogy may also be more highly valued. In the early stages of your academic career, take the time to know your institution, decide whether it's a fit with your personal and professional goals, and plan your research agenda accordingly (see Figure 4.1).

Successful midcareer academicians enjoy an enviable freedom in pursuing their research. Once the concern about tenure has been removed from the list of motivations, the research world is literally your oyster. Now is the time to pursue interdisciplinary and joint (if this was frowned on in the pretenure stage) projects, to write the great American textbook or novel, to plunge into the depths of cyberspace. Now you can begin to take risks, redefine your personal vision of the relationship between research and teaching—branch out! The faculty member who was unable to participate in writing this handbook because his dean told him it was too far afield to further his tenure case might reconsider his options at midcareer.

As a senior faculty member, take the time to mentor the junior faculty member seeking your guidance. You can be instrumental in helping to establish a probationary faculty's research agenda and helping that person navigate the political waters of the department and the institution. This collaborative relationship can provide a most satisfying cap-

Rank in order of importance, desirability, fit, and reality for you and your institution.
- Book
- Textbook
- Edited book
- Bibliography
- Article in refereed scholarly journal
- Article in refereed practical journal
- Published review
- Article in scholarly association newsletter
- Article in the popular press
- Web-based or electronic activity
  Article in e-journal (many are now peer reviewed)
  Web page creation
  Syllaweb
  Materials development
  Scholarly database
  On-line monographs
  Conversations, MOOs, MUDs

Figure 4.1. Research Agenda

stone to your own personal research agenda as you further the dissemination of knowledge in your field. Possibilities for innovation and risk taking are never greater.

Finally, keep your agenda flexible. Just as other working professionals are likely to experience several career or job changes in the course of a working lifetime, you too may find yourself seeking alternate opportunities. It can be useful to explore a variety of research venues at various points in your career. Doing so expands your horizons as well as your network. Periodically take some time to do an environmental scan of your field and the profession, as well as of your individual department and institution. Stay current regarding trends and future directions in higher education and adjust your agenda accordingly. At all levels, engage your students in your research. This practice carries a number of benefits: The student gains training in research methodology; you gain valuable assistance; and, perhaps most important, you stay in touch with higher education's primary constituency (see Figure 4.2).

❖ GETTING PUBLISHED

Resources and advice on *how* to get published and *where* to publish—conditions that vary from institution to institution—are generally available from a variety of sources, but the most easily accessible is your own

- Know your institution
- Establish a research agenda
- Educate yourself on trends in higher education
- Read practical publications
- Network
- Discuss your research with colleagues in your institutions
- Don't get bogged down in administrative duties
- Avoid vanity presses
- Make sure your research is portable
- Involve your students in your research

Figure 4.2. Faculty Research Tips

department or institution—yet another reason to take the time to understand the culture of your institution! Talk to senior faculty members, department chairs, and colleagues. Network within your institution as well as within your discipline.

In the world outside your academy, volunteer in professional organizations and for editorial boards and the like. Join or become active in consortia of several institutions, especially if you are in a small department or at a small college or university. (This project, e.g., is the result of collaboration among individuals from a consortium of colleges and universities.) Finally, seek outside sources of practical advice. Several Sage publications are dedicated to this topic. Consult the end of this chapter.

In general, if you've got a tenure clock ticking with fairly substantial research requirements attached, when in doubt focus on publishing articles in first- and second-tier refereed journals—publications that have been defined as the "sine qua non of academic scholarly attainment" (Thyer, 1994, p. 3). These tend to be highly valued by promotion and tenure committees and are less time-consuming than book projects. If you are at a teaching institution, and the powers that tenure and promote are truly committed to that philosophy, you may want to consider publishing in areas that are clearly informed by and affect your teaching. "Introductory texts and survey books, while not traditional research, represent syntheses of the current state of knowledge in a broad area" (Whicker et al., 1993, p. 74). Make sure, however, before you plunge into this area. At one member institution of a regional consortium where successful publishing was rewarded with a monetary bonus, a faculty member who wrote a biology textbook was denied the bonus because her publication was not considered "sufficiently rigorous."

❖ GETTING FUNDED

Some institutions have explicit or implicit expectations for outside funding as part of the research requirement. Find out whether your institution
has any support personnel dedicated to research funding. Many do have
built-in mechanisms for helping you get funded. In some cases, it may
be an office of one person that can serve only as a clearinghouse for
funding possibilities. In other cases, especially at large research institutions, there is a fully staffed office of sponsored research. Even in the case
of fully staffed offices, faculty may find that they are largely left to their
own devices for all but compliance issues. One faculty member from a
research institution comments, "We have an office of sponsored research.
They view their job as controlling every research project on campus. I
find them to be less than helpful; I know of some faculty who will do
anything to avoid working with them." That and similar sentiments
regarding the frustrations of working with such offices are echoed
among faculty from various institutions. Nevertheless, a most useful and
comprehensive publication, *Applying for Research Funding* (Ries & Leukefeld, 1995), grew out of an effective and successful collaboration between
faculty and staff in the office of sponsored research and programs; such
offices are essential if compliance issues are significant.

Often institutions earmark internal funds for faculty research and
development initiatives. Find out what these are and how to go about
getting them. A list of previously funded projects and a political reading
of current initiatives might help you determine not only how to get some
support for your research time, but also which of your own research
interests would be most favorably viewed at your institution—an important consideration in fleshing out your own research agenda.

In general, the smaller and the more focused on teaching the institution is, the less likely there will be an effective support mechanism for
helping you get funded. If you are on your own, or if your office is not
particularly helpful, invest some time in funding research. Numerous
publications exist regarding funding sources, and publications of most
professional organizations regularly announce discipline-specific funding opportunities. *Applying for Research Funding* (Ries & Leukefeld, 1995)
is a particularly useful resource and contains an excellent bibliography
and source list.

Remember, however, that funding that results in publication is more likely to count heavily toward promotion and tenure.

❖ RESEARCH EFFORTS IN CYBERSPACE

It's difficult to know for certain whether the countless hours you spend on electronic efforts will be rewarded with the granting of tenure or promotion, even if they initially appear to be valued at the departmental or institutional level. The debate is certainly raging and has reached the highest levels of discussion. The *Chronicle of Higher Education* has dedicated considerable attention to the topic and even established an on-line colloquy on the topic. One of the respondents, Daniel Otieno, a PhD candidate at Seton Hall University, notes, "With the proliferation of the use of computer technology in teaching in the '90s, it just makes sense to recognize application of computer technology in teaching for tenure and promotion." The Website "Professional Recognition: Technology in the Humanities" is dedicated exclusively to these issues and provides useful links to related sites as well as an opportunity to enter the discussion and help draft policy statements.

According to the *Chronicle,* many professors believe they are being denied tenure because of the time and effort they devote to electronic publishing and instructional methods (see Guernsey, 1997). Even in cases where electronic innovation is a reality and, in fact, is encouraged, using electronic publications as part of a research portfolio could prove to be problematic:

> As academe's gatekeepers grapple with such issues, professors vying for tenure, and graduate students hunting for jobs, face choices that could catapult or cripple their careers. Creating an Internet project might mark them as innovators who can take a department soaring with them into new areas of teaching and research. Or it might land them on the wrong side of a yawning divide, no longer able to communicate the value of their accomplishments to colleagues. (Guernsey, 1997, pp. A21-A22)

There is preliminary indication, however, that, in some arenas at least, scholarly efforts in cyberspace are being rewarded.

> Despite his editing an on-line journal called *Postmodern Culture*—and despite the university's reputation as a nurturing environment for electronic publishing—Dr. Unsworth had to fight for tenure. After two rounds with the committee and a long talk with the dean of arts and sciences, he was finally awarded tenure last summer. "As far as I know," he says, "I'm the first person to be tenured in an English department for doing electronic, computer-based scholarship." (Guernsey, 1997, p. A21)

If, as Ernest Boyer (1990) suggests in his landmark treatise *Scholarship Reconsidered*, innovation is to be rewarded rather than restricted (p. 80), then quality efforts involving Web-based research, publication, and instructional technologies ought to be considered among the criteria for research and teaching. The Modern Language Association (MLA) published a persuasive policy statement on this issue in April 1996. MLA's guidelines are an outgrowth of the 1993 Statement on Computer Support: "Generating, gathering, and analyzing texts electronically is becoming a necessity for all education, especially for the contributions made by the humanities" (MLA Guidelines, 1997).

The State University of New Jersey at Rutgers (1997) has taken a leading role in institutionalizing policies and procedures for evaluating electronic publishing and tenure. Rutgers' *Report of the Committee on Electronic Publishing and Tenure* contains perhaps the most comprehensive description and evaluation of scholarly publishing in the electronic environment. It also contains a fairly comprehensive list of e-journals across the disciplines. The Rutgers committee report concludes,

> The committee regards electronic dissemination as having all the capabilities to be as legitimate a form of publication as print. We urge a focus on content and quality review processes rather than on medium or format, and we suggest flexibility and common sense in interpreting the value of new publication modes.

The committee report recommends,

> Electronic publication should be considered to be an appropriate means of scholarly, artistic and professional communication, as are other means of presentation such as print and performance. . . . The content of electronic publication should be evaluated within the traditions and habits of each discipline as publication traditionally has been in other media.

- Professional Recognition: Technology in the Humanities
  http://www.rpi.edu/doherm/recognition/

- MLA Guidelines for Evaluating Computer-Related Work in the Modern Languages
  Site appended 21 May 1997
  http://www.rpi.edu/doherm/recognition/mla.html

- CoverWeb Tenure and Technology: New Values, New Guidelines
  http://english.ttu.edu/kairos/2.1/coverweb/bridge.html

- Kairos. A Journal for Teachers of Writing in Webbed Environments
  http://english.ttu.edu/kairos/

- The Chronicle of Higher Education Colloquy
  http://chronicle.com/colloquy/97/techten/techten.html

- Recognition: New Technologies, New Environments, New Scholarship and the
  Academic Work Value System
  http://www.missouri.edu/sevenc/recognition.html

- The RhetNet Defense: A New Academic Forum Toward "Shooting Hoops"
  http://www.missouri.edu/rhetnet/hoops

- A Journal for Teachers of Writing in Webbed Environments
  http://english.ttu.edu/kairos/

- Lingua MOO. An Academic Virtual Community
  http://lingua.utdallas.edu/

- The State University of New Jersey at Rutgers—Report of the Committee on
  Electronic Publishing and Tenure
  http://aultnis.rutgers.edu/texts/ept.html

- The Conference on College Composition and Communication Committee on
  Computers in Composition
  http://www.missouri.edu/sevenc/index.html

- Haynes, C., & Holmevik, J. R. (Eds.). (1997). *High wired: On the design, use, and theory of educational MOOs.* Ann Arbor: University of Michigan Press.

Figure 4.3. Web-Based Resources and Discussions

The Rutgers (1997) report together with MLA's (1997) *Guidelines for Evaluating Computer-Related Work in the Modern Languages* and numerous other on-line discussions of the topic (see Figure 4.3) provide a convincing paradigm for evaluating electronic publication and a persuasive argument for the need to do so.

What's the bottom line on Web-based publishing? Currently there appears to be a disconnect between the view of the university system in the United States as "cutting edge" in terms of research and the reluctance to accept Web-based research and publications in many institutions. On the positive side, we have at least one established university press handing out book contracts to experts in the field (Haynes & Holmevik, 1997). Although there are definite signs of change, be sure to stay tuned to the debate. In the meantime, do what you can to educate your colleagues, department, and campus.

Take the time to know your institution and where it and higher education in general are headed. There is evidence that these efforts will be more highly valued in the future. If you are a first-year faculty member, there may be time. If you are in your fourth or fifth year, you may want to be sure you include some traditional research in your portfolio.

❖ CONCLUSION

Part of what energizes us as faculty is the research we pursue in our disciplines. For many, this takes the form of highly specialized investigation into a particular area of intellectual inquiry. For others, this results in applied scholarship related to our roles as teachers. Sometimes we are engaged in efforts that fulfill a need but don't fit the existing reward structures of our institutions. Nevertheless, there is a climate of change in institutions of higher learning in the United States and a call to innovation that is echoing through campuses nationwide. Our research agendas can help shape that call as we continue to involve ourselves in the discussion.

❖ REFERENCES

Boyer, E. L. (1990). *Scholarship reconsidered: Priorities of the professorate*. Princeton, NJ: Carnegie Foundation for the Advancement of Teaching.

Clark, B. R. (1995). *Places of inquiry: Research and advanced education in modern universities*. Berkeley: University of California Press.

Guernsey, L. (1997, June 6). Scholars who work with technology fear they suffer in tenure review. *Chronicle of Higher Education*, pp. A21-A22.

Haynes, C., & Holmevik, J. R. (1997). *High wired: On the design, use, and theory of educational MOOs*. Ann Arbor: University of Michigan Press.

MLA guidelines for evaluating computer-related work in the modern languages. (1997). http://www.rpi.edu/doherm/recognition/mla.html

Ries, J. B., & Leukefeld, C. G. (1995). *Applying for research funding*. Thousand Oaks, CA: Sage.

State University of New Jersey at Rutgers. (1997). *Report of the committee on electronic publishing and tenure.* New Brunswick: Author.

Thyer, B. A. (1994). *Successful publishing in scholarly journals*. Thousand Oaks, CA: Sage.

Whicker, M. L., Kronenfeld, J. J., & Strickland, R. A. (1993). *Getting tenure*. Thousand Oaks, CA: Sage.

❖ SUGGESTED READINGS

Cahn, S. M. (Ed.). (1990). *Morality, responsibility, and the university: Studies in academic ethics.* Philadelphia: Temple University Press.

Clark, B. R. (1983). *The higher education system*. Berkeley: University of California Press.

Clark, B. R. (Ed.). (1987). *The academic profession: National, disciplinary, and institutional settings*. Berkeley: University of California Press.

Haworth, J. G., & Conrad, F. C. (1997). *Emblems of quality in higher education*. Boston: Allyn & Bacon.

Smedley, C. S., & Allen, M. (1993). *Getting your book published*. Thousand Oaks, CA: Sage.

Touraine, A. (1997). *The academic system in American society*. New Brunswick, NJ: Transaction.

5

University Service

William J. A. Marshall

Dost thou love life? Then do not squander time . . . the stuff of which life is made.

—Ben Franklin

The academy's age-old litany of teaching, scholarship, and service holds something in common with a three-legged stool. Architecturally, the tripod design forms the steadiest of platform surfaces, no leg being more important or less important than another. Academically, however, these three components of faculty workloads are by no means made out to be of equal importance. Each campus invests these three components with specific meanings, expectations, and valuative criteria.

Campus communities experience stress when there is a gap between the perceptions of what the administration says it wants from the faculty and what the faculty, in turn, produce to meet those expectations. Evaluation of faculty performance—especially for the wobbly legged tenure-track probationers—hinges on an evolving series of interactive communications. Because not all chairs and deans are either able or willing to communicate clearly what is expected of probationary faculty, then it is up to the deans to pull from the chairs what needs further explication.

Ultimately, such communication establishes not only *what* the administration expects but also *how* and *when* it will inspect what it expects of the faculty being evaluated.

Diamond (1995), for example, recommends that teaching be 50% of what a faculty member does, with the remainder being divided between scholarship and service—though not necessarily in equal amounts. Clausen (1996) believes teaching and scholarship to be complementary activities when he states that "while research activity does not guarantee effective teaching, it greatly enhances a faculty member's understanding of a discipline" (p. 44). As for the remaining member of the triad—service—both authors agree that although it can never outweigh teaching and scholarship, its absence can seriously compromise the sociopolitical milieu that enters into the peer-driven tenure review process.

The purpose of this chapter is to assist the fledgling tenure-track faculty member with the art of juggling the demands of classroom teaching and scholarship, on the one hand, with the demands of service, on the other hand, as they become spliced into the wedges of an ever-diminishing time pie. Whereas the cerebral achievements of classroom teaching and scholarship lend themselves to easily identifiable sources of documentation—for example, student and peer evaluations of teaching, refereed publications, and productions—the time investment demanded of service can almost approach the point of diminishing returns if not handled with sagacity. This chapter sets forth a dispassionate analysis of the service area sector with recommendations on how to couple efficient time management skills with effective political management skills that can be conducive to the achievement of a superior faculty evaluation rating. The chapter's focus—moving from the concept of service in general to the application of governance-related university service in particular—provides a fitting companion piece to Chapter 6, "Professional Service." Both chapters, when taken together, round out the entirety of the service arena.

❖ TIME MANAGEMENT SKILLS

> Time is the coin of our life . . . the only coin we have. And we should be the only ones who determine how to spend it. If we be not careful, others will spend it for us!
>
> —Carl Sandburg

Time is a happening that affects us all. We may think that we are just *passing time,* when all the while time is passing us at a rate of 60 seconds per minute. We may lose our wealth, our money, and our friends and still be able to recoup our losses; yet, if we lose a stretch of time, we have lost that forever. Consider the popular refrain "I do not have enough time." How absurd! Each and every one of us has all the time in the world—a constant of 24 hours per day. Hence, *running out of time* is not the problem, but *running into activities* that willy-nilly consume this precious resource is the problem. So it is not *time traps* that we must be wary of, but *activity traps.* And the resource arena is replete with them.

"I can't keep up with my profession and my life—my workload is too heavy. I cannot possibly finish my work by the end of the day, the semester, or the academic year," writes Gmelch (1996, p. 22) in recounting the travails of tenured full professors looking for a way out of their classic activity traps. If the full professors are being swallowed up in this activity trap morass, then how much more so are the tenure-track professors?

The 19th-century Italian economist Vilfredo Pareto, pondering the problem of productivity payoffs, hypothesized that 80% of our achievements come from 20% of our focused efforts. Consequently, it is important that we identify that time zone of our ordinary working day where we hit our stride, getting the most bang for the buck. This mind-set forces us to choose, and to choose wisely. A *time decision* is a behavioral decision, a statement about our values and our priorities. The way we spend our time defines the activities we value in our life. If the activities we engage in contribute to our goal of attaining tenure and promotion, then we are using our time effectively. And if our pragmatic grasp of the Pareto Principle enables us to intensify the focus of our time on task, then we are also using our time efficiently. This combined skill of being effective while simultaneously demonstrating the ability to manage professional time and personal time efficiently is a sine qua non for success in any line of work, especially during the probationary period of the professorate. It is not time that we must learn to manage, but self.

The writings of both Shelton and Skaggs (1996) and Blackburn and Lawrence (1995) illustrate the critical intersection of time management skills with the on-the-job demands of the academy. For example, Shelton and Skaggs (1996) state, "We know a great deal about how much time faculty devote to teaching, research, and service; how time spent in any one of these activities is related to time spent in others; and how time expenditures vary by institutional and individual characteristics" (p. 16). They note that although faculty members who teach more tend to publish less, the distinctions between the tenure-track and tenured faculty across all professional ranks hold constant. That is, 40% of assistant professors, associate professors, and full professors devote significant segments of their time to preparing for class, upgrading their class materials, and developing new courses.

This is encouraging news for probationary faculty, knowing that the lion's share of their current time pies—teaching—is not unique to their beginner's status but is characteristic of the very reason why they were called to this profession in the first place—the love of teaching. On the downside, however, this becomes a cautionary matter for tenure track-ers. The time-consuming nature of teaching-related activities seldom results in publication, frequently defies documentation, and almost never lends itself to measurable outcomes. Be that as it may, such pedagogical pursuits greatly contribute to the lifeblood of intellectual life on the campus. Without it, would we continue to have a community of scholars? Without it, would our students continue to flock to our classrooms with motivation and enthusiasm? Without it, would we—as teachers—continue in our roles as being the first student in our very own classrooms?

Let us metamorphose the image of our round-topped three-legged stool and imagine it as a metaphor that captures the essence of what we are about in higher education. What we have before us is the image of a teaching leg, a scholarship leg, and a service leg all fitting together, as finely crafted tenons, into the underside mortise joints of a madly spin-ning clock. And though we may be spin doctors in the political arena, the only spin control we have available to us in the temporal arena is to realize that our time decisions are behavioral decisions, loudly announc-ing the values and priorities we have invested in on our activities. The rest of the chapter examines the effectiveness of the choice of selective activities as it applies to the politically rich service sector arena.

❖ POLITICAL MANAGEMENT SKILLS

The whole point of getting things done is knowing what to leave undone.
—Lady Reading of Great Britain

Institutional priorities vary according to campus culture, mandated missions, and budgetary climates. Professional priorities, however, vary according to the predilection of faculty members for becoming involved in what comes natural or easy for them. The personality literature and the time management literature converge on this so-called priorities principle; namely, that people tend to do things that they enjoy first, before doing things they find themselves not to enjoy. Take for example extraverts. They enjoy being with people. They need to be with people because that is how they stay energized. Introverts, on the other hand, experience a draining of energy when being with people. For them, energy flows from reading alone, thinking alone, and meditating alone—the very things that induce restlessness, lassitude, and energy drain in extraverts. Keirsey and Bates (1984) and Choiniere and Keirsey (1992) contrast the gregarious and assertive characteristics of extroverts with the more attentive and isolative characteristics of intraverts. These attitudinal preferences for dealing with the outside world affect our time decisions and—if left unchecked—can impair our overall effectiveness.

Clausen (1996) waxes poetic when he describes the unacceptability of ignoring any sector of the customary faculty workload by stating that "the faculty workload combining teaching, scholarship, and service represents a seamless garment whose sleeves and hems cannot profitably be evaluated apart from the whole gown" (p. 43). He cites instances of faculty colleagues who do little, if any, service sector work—no matter the attendant difficulties this may impose on other members of the department, school, or institution. This plaint is not what this chapter is about, however. This dearth of service sector work is not the danger to beware of, for probationary members of a department's faculty. Instead, the danger is too much involvement with the activities falling in this sector of work. Too much attendance, for example, to the needs of peer review of all kinds—a.k.a. committee work. Too much attendance, for example, to the political demands of shared governance—demands that periodically siphon off the psychic energies needed for teaching and publishing. And, too much attendance, for example, to the allure of professional association responsibilities and community outreach activities.

There's an old saying to the effect that any fool can start a love affair, but as for breaking one off, that's something else again. Likewise for tenure-track faculty members who traipse through the treacherous sands of this time-sensitive sector of service without so much as a thought for what they are getting in return for their enormous expenditure of energy and time. Invariably, what swallows up their effectiveness and ultimately their ticket to tenure and promotion is the black hole of meetings. Incompetent meeting management is endemic to academe. Meetings, bereft of beginnings and endings, leave the unwary wandering with scant sense of purpose, closure, or accomplishment.

Given this dismal swamp, Herculean efforts must be made to engage in only those service sector activities delivering the biggest bang for the buck. The remainder of this chapter will help both tenure-track faculty and tenured faculty alike increase their effectiveness in achieving their professional goals of tenure, promotion, and acclaim.

❖ SERVICE ACTIVITIES

As representative of most writers on the subject, Tucker (1984) operationally describes the service sector as embracing only those activities that directly relate to the faculty member's field of expertise and to the institution's statement of mission. Building on Tucker, one can induce a set of generic examples of these activities to include

- involvement in department, school, and university-wide committees or the faculty senate;
- involvement with appropriate professional organizations;
- involvement in organizing and expediting meetings, conferences, and workshops;
- involvement in media efforts focusing on the institution or profession; and
- involvement with local, state, and national boards, commissions, or agencies.

Such activity genres arrange themselves differently for each institution along a continuum of relative levels of importance. Some institutions do not even classify all these listed activities as being exclusive to the service sector. For example, involvement with appropriate professional organizations may be categorized by some schools and departments as falling under the aegis of scholarship—depending on both the academic discipline and the nature of the professional involvement.

Aside from such differences of kind, we also have to recognize the existence of some very real differences of degree. That is, service sector activity genres align themselves vertically along a continuum of relative importance simply because some roles command more respect than others by virtue of their very nature. These degrees of perceived relative importance are usually a function of (a) the roles assigned, (b) the performance within the roles assigned, and (c) the value the department and school ascribe to such roles and performance indicators. Recognition of this vertical dimension by tenure-track faculty members effectively increases their likelihood of getting the most bang for the buck. Why? Because the nature of some roles—being more visible and prestigious than others—makes more public the display of superior performance. Contrariwise, the demonstration of superior performance in lower-profile backwater roles provides an inefficient buck without a bang.

As a case in point, Tucker (1984) developed a system of weights that assigns a higher value to service on a university-wide committee—for example, 5 points—versus service on a national committee—for example, 3 points. Tucker's system assigns a role differential of 10 points for *chairing* the former and 5 points for *chairing* the latter. Whether or not a faculty member gets the entire allocation of points depends on evidence of visible performance within the role assigned. An extrapolated summary of his system serves the purpose of identifying activities that deliver the most bang for the buck (cf. pp. 164-165). Keeping in mind that each institution adjusts the weights to its own mission and needs and that each academic department further adjusts the weights to fit the accustomed practices of the academic discipline, Tucker's activity genres and suggested weights (in parentheses) are shown in Table 5.1.

Table 5.1 provides the closest approximation we have for the development of a taxonomy of high-impact service-related categories that maximize a fledgling faculty member's political capital. Such capital provides a much-needed return on investment for the precious time that would ordinarily have been given to scholarly writing deadlines and demanding teaching schedules. Such capital may also psychologically influence the swing vote of members serving on tenure and promotion committees. The legends and lore of such campus committees denying to well-published scholars and well-liked classroom teachers their much-deserved promotions or their coveted tenure appointments are legendary. Such ephemeral rationales as personality quirks or gender biases

Table 5.1 Tucker's (1984) Suggested Weights and Activities

Committee Activities	Professional Activities
(10) Chair of a universitywide committee	(05) Chair of a national committee
(05) Member of a universitywide committee	(03) Member of a national committee
(05) Chair of a schoolwide committee	(03) Chair of a state committee
(03) Member of a schoolwide committee	(01) Member of a state committee
[10]* [Chair of the faculty senate]	(07) Officer of professional organization
(07) Member of faculty senate	(03) Leader of in-service workshop
(05) Chair of search committee	(05) Organizer of workshop
(03) Member of search committee	(01) Member of professional organization

*Extrapolation by author.

or "just-doesn't-fit-within-the-team" assessments have unofficially contributed to the demise of otherwise promising careers in academe. As Wilson (1997) notes, "Even though a majority of the faculty in a department may vote in favor of a [well-respected female] candidate for tenure, there may be people in the minority who have access to folks higher up" (p. A-10), thereby jettisoning the process.

Exposure gained within the campus governance system and performance recognized within an increasing series of service role assignments, on and off campus, effectively contribute to a successful career in any profession. Politics can never be divorced from any people-related decision in any organization. When we consider how finicky, persnickety, and unpredictable a faculty organization can be, then it becomes all the more imperative to learn the ropes as quickly as possible. You don't think so? Ask any campus administrator. Ask any aggrieved member of the faculty. Finally, ask yourself: "Can I afford to go it alone with so much at stake?"

❖ THE PERFORMANCE PORTFOLIO

Forewarned is forearmed. To reduce the anxiety borne of uncertainty and to map the strategies aimed at success, Seldin (1997) provides a practical guide for improving the probability of success for a faculty member moving through the crinkum-crankum turns of the tenure promotion process. Seldin provides to both administrators and faculty a pragmatic and research-based methodology for compiling a performance portfolio of accomplishments. Although the focus of his treatise is primarily on the teaching aspect of the faculty member's workload, it takes but an *in extenso* leap of logic to apply the same methodology to the remaining workload aspects of scholarship and service.

The performance portfolio assembles within a single three-ring binder evidence of teaching evaluations, copies of publications and research grants, and testimonial evidence of accomplishments and appreciation for services rendered. The portfolio approach promotes efficiency—doing things right—by documenting the daily evidence that accumulates in the life of a faculty member. Such a small investment of time per day or per week is far more preferable to the alternative of scrounging around the halls of memory and the desks of clutter at evaluation time for the evidence to justify a favorable evaluation. As cited in Seldin (1997) by a foreign language professor,

> A friend of mine who was on the selection committee said it was my [performance] portfolio that did the job. The selection committee was so impressed with the way the portfolio documented my teaching [scholarship, and service] that they had no other choice than to vote for me. (p. 253)

The performance portfolio also promotes effectiveness—doing the right things—by increasing a faculty member's sense of synchronicity with the operating standards governing the rules and regulations of the tenure and promotion committees. Diamond (1994) brilliantly describes the principles, processes, and appended guidelines for defining the parameters of scholarly work and professional service-related work within selected academic disciplines. Although Diamond addresses these issues in the abstract, it behooves new faculty members to check out in the concrete exactly how the processes of promotion and tenure review work on their own campuses. For example, "on most campuses there are distinct differences in the criteria applied for promotion and for tenure. . . . Promotion decisions focus primarily on the candidate's accomplishments to-date, [whereas] tenure considerations tend to consider carefully the candidate's . . . potential" (p. 3). However idiosyncratic the specifics of any given campus review process may be, Diamond's rendition is estimable and should be required reading for anyone working in higher education.

Like Seldin (1997), Diamond (1994) praises the role of the performance portfolio in the review process. And Diamond, even more so than Seldin, encourages the insertion of a faculty essay in the portfolio's front-end section. "While this descriptive essay may have a number of functions, its primary purpose is to provide . . . the context for the items submitted to the committee for review" (p. 18). This essay's placement within the crucially important portfolio is sound, strategic advice. This essay's narrative tells the committee how the substantive works contained within the portfolio (a) mesh with the missions of the institution, (b) mesh with the priorities of the academic department, and (c) mesh with the prevailing criteria for consideration of promotion or tenure. Finally, this essay's design encourages careful reading by the reviewers because (a) it is brief, (b) it provides a rationale for why what is there has been included, and (c) it provides a description of the conveniently tabbed contents and the sections wherein they can be found. Although the reviewers will dwell on the quality of the evidence submitted within the portfolio proper, the quality of the essay proper may significantly contribute to the context in which those self-same works will be judged. Seldin appends working examples of typical faculty performance portfolios, all of which are worthy of emulation.

Diamond (1994, cf. pp. 49-50) provides an especially helpful example of how to assemble evidence for a typical service arena activity such as serving on a community task force appointed by the mayor. His clever presentation of evidence greatly enhances the likelihood of a candidate being awarded the full complement of points recommended by Tucker (1984)—if weights are being used by the campus in question—pending, of course, the actual evidence given. A slightly modified excerpt of this example appears in Figure 5.1. I also direct the reader to *A Faculty Guide for Relating Public Service to the Promotion and Tenure Review Process* (1993) and *Professional Service and Faculty Rewards* (Elman & Smock, 1985) for further ways of assessing this difficult-to-document sector of faculty workload.

❖ FACULTY GOVERNANCE

No treatment of the service sector of faculty workloads can ever be complete without a discussion of the sine qua non that makes a univer-

Rationale
- Requires high level of disciplinary expertise
- Fits with institutional mission statement of providing community service
- Provides case study material for classroom and further research

Evidence of Documentation
- Essay describes the problem addressed, the role played, and the lessons learned
- Essay describes specific actions taken as part of the task force
- Transcripts of the minutes of task force meetings
- Letters of recommendation of task force chair and members
- Testimonial letters from community groups benefiting from task force work
- Course syllabus and materials resulting from this task force involvement
- Statement of institutional missions or school goals supporting this activity
- Samples of task force interviews with mayor or community leaders
- Results of task force actions, community initiatives, and accomplishments

Valuative Criteria
- Demonstrates high level of professional expertise
- Demonstrates state-of-the-art knowledge in conflict resolution strategies
- Demonstrates strong performance as task force member
- Demonstrates innovative approaches to problem solving
- Demonstrates knowledge of current community action literature
- Publishes results of activities in news media and professional journals

Figure 5.1. Service on Community Task Force Appointed by Mayor

sity a university: shared governance. This is the arena where faculty and administrators alike cut their teeth in the business of power, decision making, and campus politics. One local wag on my campus—in reaction to a particularly incompetent member of the administration—acerbically defined the term in this fashion: "Shared governance is exactly what [the administrator in question] decides to share with us." Weinstein (1993)—Moving a Battleship with Your Bare Hands: Governing a University System—balances this jaundiced aside: "If shared governance means faculty veto power over . . . administrative decisions, then—with all due respect—it is an idea whose time has passed. If, on the other hand, it means faculty will devote themselves to carrying out . . . instruction, research, and service, then shared governance . . . will keep the university [vibrant] *and responsive to the needs of students and citizens* [alike]."

The business of shared governance requires the eternal vigilance of an informed faculty in stemming the riptide tendencies of impatient, closure-seeking, power-hungry administrators who want their way and want it now! Such administrators populate the campuses of the land, never mastering the conundrum of power, which is this: The more power you allocate to the people whom you serve as an administrator, the more power they in turn will allot to you (Marshall, 1990). Such administrators have only belatedly come to realize that leading faculty is akin to steering a modern supertanker: It takes several miles of forward-steering movement before the giant ship begins to change its course. No behemoth of the seven seas and no faculty of the nation's campuses have ever, or will ever, turn on a dime.

The Association of Governing Boards of Universities and Colleges published the results of its recent blue-ribbon panel, *Reviewing the Academic Presidency: Stronger Leadership for Tougher Times* (1996). The report shows ample evidence of grasping the import of such conundrums and metaphors. It regales the reader with an amusing anecdote about a former president of Columbia University—General Dwight D. Eisenhower. One day early in his tenure as president, Eisenhower, in true military fashion, summoned his chief academic officer into his office to lay down his interpretation of the university's policies. After a respectful silence, the provost replied, "Mr. President, you must remember that the faculty *are* the university" (p. 15). The report also said that

> shared governance . . . describes a system in which boards, presidents, and faculty fully participate in making decisions about . . . issues affecting the institution. The roles of the three participants are sometimes specified, but oftentimes not. Everyone shares the tacit understanding that while the board has legal responsibility for the institution, it delegates many of its powers to the administration and faculty. This system is at the heart of the academy's governing problems. Part of this difficulty arises from the vagueness of the concept and its execution. . . . [and] (w)hatever the formal arrangements [may be], the faculty expect to be consulted on most if not all important decisions. . . . And *consultation* is often a code word for consent. (pp. 7-8)

Yes indeed, times are tougher now than ever before. The times call for the emergence of leaders from within the ranks of the faculty and the administration alike. The times call for a continuing dialogue among the members of the board, the administration, and the faculty to refine their understanding of both the concept and the execution of shared governance. As an evolving, vivifying notion, shared governance defies easy definition. For to define is, also, to delimit. Shared governance, far from being static or stagnant, requires constant nurturing, enlightened dialogue, and inviolable trust. As the players within the governance picture change on any given campus, so too will the conceptions of shared governance on that campus change.

Having served at the helm of the campus governance system at Gallaudet University for almost 10 years, I recently contributed some service sector work by helping to redraft the 1997 version of the university faculty bylaws. The preamble to those bylaws throws light on this much-needed topic of shared governance understanding:

> Gallaudet University operates in accordance with the principles of shared governance. Shared governance is a frame of mind. It is an attitude. It is a willingness to make concerted efforts to involve the right players—trustees, administrators, faculty—to unleash the collective synergy of an ongoing state of truly collaborative efforts. Shared governance is based on trust. And trust is built on a foundation of respect. Both trust and respect grow out of authenticity in our interpersonal relations with each other. Truly, shared governance—the sine qua non of academe—must be the defining characteristic of what makes Gallaudet a collegial university. (p. i)

❖ SCENARIOS

Before I close, allow me to dwell on the twin concerns of efficiency—doing things right—and effectiveness—doing the right things—by applying the principles of each to some typical academic scenarios. Seldom, if ever, is the challenge to balance the seesaw of efficiency-effectiveness a binary, either-or type of decision. Instead, it is a shrewd challenge to balance this yin and yang coupling to further one's chances for tenure and promotion.

Scenario A

A newly reappointed assistant professor—still 4 years away from his tenure evaluation—was informed by his department chair to start developing some visibility in the department and on the campus by volunteering for some service sector activities. Up until now, he had been concentrating on teaching activities —understandably so. His colleagues suggested that the usual route to election on campus governance bodies was to volunteer services so that people could get to know him. After all, no one votes for an unknown.

Considering the possibilities, the assistant professor began considering both his class teaching schedule and his need to be home early on the afternoons that his wife had to work the night shift as an intensive care nurse at the local hospital. The only realistic volunteer service options he had open to him were the following:

1. *The faculty welfare committee, meeting every Monday from 2:00 to 5:00 p.m.—due to its enormous backlog, and in much need of volunteers to work on its many task forces;*
2. *The committee on budget and finance, meeting every other Wednesday in a brown bag lunch format for the purpose of advising the administration on parity issues, benefits packages, and annual cost-of-living adjustments; and*
3. *The committee on faculty development, meeting no more than six times a year and charged with the responsibility for awarding a total of $45,000 to faculty submitting competitive proposals for small grants to further professional development.*

From a time-clock perspective, the assistant professor had no scheduling conflicts with any of these options. From a political perspective, he considered the pros and cons of each. Option 1 he saw as a stepping stone to eventual election to the faculty senate. Option 2 he saw as an avenue to get to meet with the provost—to whom all recommendations were made by the committee. And Option 3 he realized to be a minefield, because he heard some of the senior members of his department grumbling about how their proposals had been turned down by the committee last year.

What would your advice be if you were his mentor?

Scenario B

A tenured full professor—having been extensively involved in the campus governance system for many years, capping that enviable service record off with a 3-year stint as chair of the faculty senate—decided to shift her focus to scholarship. She resurrected her interest in studying group dynamics and started preparing a $2,200 small grants proposal. Simultaneously, she agreed to author a book chapter on conflict management, and was considering applying for a half-year sabbatical leave to do the research and the writing.

While the professor was waiting to hear word on her submitted proposal, the president requested a meeting. Having interacted with this president many times in her capacity as a governance leader, she looked forward to seeing the president again. After exchanging the usual pleasantries, the president brought the conversation around to the great respect she had for the professor's interpersonal and group leadership skills. As a consequence, the president asked her to chair a yearlong task force composed of two trustees, the provost, one academic dean, and three members of the faculty senate. Feeling flattered, the professor indicated the need for some time to mull over this offer, mentioning—as an aside—her own wishes and plans for a sabbatical.

Upon returning to her office, she sought out the advice of her department chair. Not being surprised at the president's offer, the chair confided his need to have an experienced professional head up the department's professional standard's accreditation committee within the school of education. The site visit was 21 months away. The professor was loath to turn the chair down, considering how supportive he was of her promotion last year. Her campus governance responsibilities were so demanding that she had published only modestly during that period as chair of the faculty senate. What to do?

No one else is responsible for how we use our time or how we live our life. The question is, "Do we know what we want to do with the rest of our life?" For dilemmas such as this, an appointment with ourselves becomes the first order of business. Difficult? Not if we grasp the import of Seneca's words: "It is not because things are difficult that we do not dare; it is because we do not dare that they are difficult."

❖ SUMMARY

Service, having perhaps been regarded as a distant country cousin to its big-city counterparts teaching and scholarship, suddenly looms as the all-important glue that holds together the whole enterprise of higher education. Without the contributions of the faculty's service to the continuing evolution and renewed understanding of shared governance, institutions of higher education would cease to exist and be replaced by market-driven, top-down hierarchical learning corporations. Can we afford to let this happen? If not, then consider the most effective ways that your contributory political management skills can effect a vibrant shared governance climate on your campus. And in so doing, live out the words of Professor Louis Pasteur: "The most effective gift we can make to our time and place is the gift of a creative and constructive life."

❖ REFERENCES

Association of Governing Boards of Universities and Colleges. (1996). *Reviewing the academic presidency: Stronger leadership for tougher times.* Washington, DC: Author.

Blackburn, R. T., & Lawrence, J. H. (1995). *Faculty at work.* Baltimore: Johns Hopkins University.

Choiniere, R., & Keirsey, D. (1992). *Presidential temperament.* Del Mar, CA: Prometheus Nemesis.

Clausen, C. (1996). Faculty workloads and legislative curiosity. *Academe, 82*(5), 40-44.

Diamond, R. (1994). *Serving on promotion and tenure committees: A faculty guide.* Boston: Anker.

Diamond, R. M. (1995). *Preparing for promotion and tenure review: A faculty guide.* Boston: Anker.

Elman, S. E., & Smock, S. M. (1985). *Professional service and faculty rewards: Toward an integrated structure.* Washington, DC: National Association of State Universities and Land-Grant Colleges.

A faculty guide for relating public service to the promotion and tenure review process. (1993). Champaign: University of Illinois Office of Continuing Education.

Gmelch, W. H. (1996). It's about time. *Academe, 82*(5), 22-27.

Keirsey, D., & Bates, M. (1984). *Please understand me: Character & temperament types.* Del Mar, CA: Gnosology Books.

Marshall, W. J. A. (1990). Power: An administrator's guide along the corridors of arrogance. *ERIC Administrator's Update, 7*(1-3), 1-12.

Seldin, P. (1997). *The teaching portfolio: A practical guide to improved performance and promotion/tenure decisions* (2nd ed.). Boston: Anker.

Shelton, B. A., & Skaggs, S. (1996). How faculty members spend their time: A closer look. *Academe, 82*(5), 16-21.

Tucker, A. (1984). *Chairing the academic department: Leadership among peers* (2nd ed.). New York: Macmillan.

Weinstein, L. A. (1993). *Moving a battleship with your bare hands: Governing a university system.* Madison, WI: Magna.

Wilson, R. (1997, June 6). At Harvard, Yale, and Stanford, women lose tenure bids despite backing from departments. *Chronicle of Higher Education,* p. A-10.

6

Professional Service

Karen L. Medsker

The role of professional service in your career is a unique and important one. Although service is often viewed as less important than research and teaching, it can actually be the catalyst that brings excitement and coherence to other faculty roles. For some faculty members, professional service is the most interesting and rewarding aspect of their careers. Professional service encompasses activities that are rich and varied in their content, that are performed for and with diverse people and organizations, that provide opportunities for personal growth and creativity, and that often enhance, directly or indirectly, teaching, research, or other aspects of the faculty member's life. In some cases, the rewards are moral and spiritual, because charitable causes and social justice activities can be incorporated into one's professional life.

To ensure that your professional service activities are optimally productive and rewarding, however, you should match them to your professional goals and carefully select them to maximize the return on your time investment. Extensive advice on both political and time management skills related to service is presented in Chapter 5, "University Service."

Chapter 5 presents a broad view of service, with emphasis on service to one's own institution. This chapter focuses on professional service, defined here as service (primarily unpaid) to professional societies, government at all levels, schools, other nonprofit agencies, or the public. Professional service uses professional skills or some extension of them. For example, if you are a law professor, professional services can be legal or related services, and for the art professor, professional services can be artistic. In this chapter, then, professional service is distinguished from what may be called "community service," in which the law professor plays violin in a community orchestra or the art professor serves food at a soup kitchen. Consulting (work done outside the university for pay) is considered different from professional service, but the two may overlap at times. For example, consulting done at a significantly reduced rate for a charitable organization may be seen as partly professional service, and honoraria may be paid for speaking or review activities not primarily done for financial compensation.

Note that universities categorize faculty activities differently. Some of the activities referred to here as professional service (e.g., member of a research committee of a professional society) may be considered scholarship in some schools but service in others. Some institutions may not distinguish among professional service, community service, and university service, simply categorizing all as service. To compete successfully in your own institution's rank and tenure system, be sure to find out the nature, quality, and quantity of activities required either formally or informally by the culture.

Consider these scenarios based on the experiences of actual faculty members.

Scenario A

George is a professor of computer science whose university is located in a major city. At a professional computer science conference, George met a colleague who works as a volunteer in the city's public schools helping kids learn to use computers. They discussed the problems of involving precollege students in computer science, particularly low-income and minority students. (Typically,

*computer science majors tend to be white Americans or international students.)
As a result, they designed and implemented a program in which a group of
university professors, high school teachers, and middle school teachers work
throughout the school year with precollege students on projects related to
computer science, then provide the students an opportunity to present the results
of their projects at a conference held on the university campus. The conference
provides a goal, as well as a recognition opportunity, for their hard work.*

*Everyone involved, including the proud parents who attend the conference,
has found the program to be rich and rewarding. Some of George's university
students gained practical teaching experience and the rewards of serving others.
Several former secondary school participants are now pursuing higher education
or careers in computer science. George himself has benefited in several ways. He
feels good about helping students enter a challenging career field they might not
otherwise have considered possible. His activities "count" toward his professional service requirement each year at performance review time. The university
appreciates this contribution toward its image as a partner in the community.
In addition, two of the former program participants are now members of George's
undergraduate research group, helping George further his own research interests
and prepare projects for publication and presentation. George's track record of
community involvement can be used in writing grant proposals.*

Scenario B

*Emily and Steve, who both teach research and evaluation methods in a university
school of education, were asked to help a local county government. The department of parks and recreation wanted to evaluate its summer camp program to
improve the program and enhance enrollments. (The two faculty members were
offered modest compensation for their efforts, but much less than they might have
earned in a regular consulting job.) Emily and Steve worked for several months
with a team from the department to plan the study, design the survey instruments, train the data gathering team, collect and analyze the data, and present
the results to county decision makers. In the end, the department found several
ways to improve the summer camp program, including some ideas it had not
previously considered, and a plan was put in place to increase enrollments. Emily
and Steve's dean received a letter of commendation for their personnel files. In
addition, the two faculty members wrote a paper about the project for a nonref-*

ereed journal summarizing practical tips based on lessons learned. A final benefit for Emily and Steve was that, through the connections they made with county employees, they were able to place a graduate intern there and provide several real-life class projects for their students.

Scenario C

Suzanne is a business school professor in a small Midwestern university town. Specializing in human resource management, Suzanne is active in the Society for Human Resource Management (SHRM). She is a member both of the international organization and her local chapter, which she helped found. During the past several years, Suzanne has volunteered a great deal of time to SHRM. She has served as an officer and board member of the local chapter and actively recruits her graduate students to join the chapter and attend program meetings, at which she and they have also been speakers. Suzanne is also a member of the editorial board of SHRM's scholarly journal and regularly reviews articles submitted for publication. This past year, she also served as a reviewer of instructional materials produced by SHRM to help professionals study for professional certification exams. She has served on national committees to plan various aspects of the annual conference.

Suzanne feels that she has gained a great deal from her SHRM volunteer activities. Not only does she keep up with new developments in her field, which she can build into her teaching plans, but she also rubs elbows with other society leaders and makes valuable contacts. Suzanne has achieved a reputation within the society as a specialist in executive compensation, which means she has been asked to be a member or moderator of panel discussions at local and regional conferences and to edit a special issue of the journal. She recently joined two other active SHRM members in conducting a survey of best business practices in the executive compensation area, and they expect to publish their results as well as prepare a report for SHRM. All in all, Suzanne finds that her SHRM activities contribute to her professional development and build her portfolio of experience in all three areas of teaching, research, and service.

❖ SERVICE TO PROFESSIONAL SOCIETIES

Perhaps the most obvious and readily available opportunity for professional service is involvement with a professional society in your academic field. These organizations depend heavily on volunteers to accomplish their goals and welcome your support. Figure 6.1 presents a wide range, but only a sample, of possible ways to participate actively. Although the activities are divided into three categories, some activities may belong to more than one category. Depending on the nature and size of the society, many additional opportunities are available. If you are relatively new to your profession or to a geographic area, the best way to get involved is to attend local chapter meetings—and be sure to be there for the networking sessions. Join a committee and volunteer for tasks. You will not be a stranger for very long, and you will easily find out what other opportunities are the best match for your interests. The next step is to become a leader at the local level. Chairing committees or serving as an officer leads directly to involvement at the national or international level.

❖ SERVICE TO GOVERNMENT

Another possible venue for professional service is government agencies. Pro bono or reduced-fee consulting is possible in almost every academic discipline, and government agencies (local, state, and federal) exist everywhere. Generally, government agencies are studded with experts (as well as "generalist bureaucrats"). These experts, dedicated to public service and the pursuit of knowledge but often lacking in time to do any or all the research or creative activity they would like to do, often make excellent professional partners for academics. They can provide exciting and worthwhile service projects for professors, while at the same time satisfying their own needs for more scholarly pursuits.

Relationships with government colleagues can benefit the faculty member in many ways, leading to additional opportunities for service, recruitment of government employees as students to the university, joint publishing opportunities, inside information on available research and

Governance Activities
- Serve on the board of directors
- Be an officer in a local chapter
- Serve on the board of a local chapter
- Help to create or revise the constitution and bylaws
- Serve on or chair a standing committee
- Be a national or international officer

Organization-Building Activities
- Start a new chapter in your city or region
- Organize or sponsor a student chapter on your campus
- Participate in or lead a membership campaign
- Participate in or lead an assessment of member needs
- Study and recommend changes in member services and benefits
- Seek out and publicize opportunities for student involvement
- Encourage and reward students for active participation
- Create a publicity video, brochure, or Web page about the society
- Start an Internet discussion group on a hot topic
- Organize a special interest group within the society that meets in person or on-line

Technical, Scholarly, and Creative Activities
- Conduct a study to answer a question or solve a problem important to the society and to your field
- Organize a local or regional conference
- Organize a new event at an existing conference
- Review proposals for papers or presentations at a national or international conference
- Head the committee to select the outstanding doctoral dissertation of the year in your field
- Create a video, brochure, or Web page about a specific issue that concerns the society or its members
- Present papers, panels, and workshops at local, regional, and national and international conferences of the society
- Submit articles to the society's journals
- Serve on the editorial board (or referee articles in your specialty area) for the society's scholarly journal
- Study and report the competencies needed by professionals in your field
- Study and recommend an academic curriculum to match the competencies
- Initiate or participate in pro bono consulting to worthwhile organizations and causes sponsored by the society

Figure 6.1. Sample Forms of Involvement in Professional Societies

development grants, consulting opportunities, class projects and internship placements for students, and government employees as potential members and volunteers for your professional society. Like contact with business and industry, government involvement also keeps you in touch with real-world issues and problems. Some examples of actual professional service to government are as follows:

- A professor of instructional design gave a seminar on training needs assessment to an interagency group of government training specialists. This 2-hour seminar led to the recruitment of an excellent adjunct instructor for the university and a consulting job for the professor. He could also list the seminar on his annual report as a service activity.

- An electrical engineering professor specializing in telecommunications frequently gives expert testimony before legislative committees and regulatory agency panels that govern long distance and local telephone rates. This experience enhances her teaching because it adds to her fund of concrete examples of how the subject matter may be applied.

- An education professor specializing in tests and measurement worked with his state department of education to help determine the kinds of achievement and competency tests to be used in the public schools and to help select the contractor who will develop the tests. Technical issues raised during this project led to a new book on academic testing coauthored by the professor and the state department official.

- A physical education faculty member volunteers with her local county government to give fitness and wellness workshops for government employees and their families. These are welcome opportunities to overcome the isolation of working in a tiny academic department in a small college. The work also has been a chance to develop her presentation skills and get ideas for case studies for a textbook she's writing.

- Academics in scientific fields often review grant proposals for the National Science Foundation, whereas those in artistic fields do the same for the National Endowment for the Arts. Sometimes connections made in this way lead to rotational or even permanent appointments within these government agencies.

One way to initiate professional contact with an agency of interest is to volunteer to give a presentation or workshop in your specialty area, either a formal seminar to government employees who are also in your specialty area or a less formal brown bag lunch session for a more general interest audience. Another avenue is to let students and colleagues know you are available, perhaps by distributing a simple brochure listing your skills or areas of expertise. You may also meet relevant government employees or officials through your professional societies, civic activities, or social contacts. Let people know what your interests and talents are, and the opportunities will come.

❖ SERVICE TO BUSINESS AND INDUSTRY

Many of the strategies and benefits related to government service also apply to business and industry. Opportunities exist to serve on advisory boards of companies. Organizations that do research and development in your field may have cooperative programs with universities or joint committees to work on industry-education relations issues. Consortia of businesses in a geographic area or economic development councils often seek cooperation and expertise from academic experts. If you need a real-world laboratory in which to test a theory or conduct an experiment, your business contacts may be able to help.

One organizational development professor, for example, studied the effects of downsizing on morale and career development in a large multinational company. She was able to complete an important phase of her research, while her data (sanitized, of course) helped the company analyze its internal problems. Connections in business and industry can have many direct and indirect benefits, including overcoming the ivory tower syndrome, meeting colleagues with complementary professional interests, promoting economic growth in your community, learning about research and development grant opportunities, finding internships and jobs for your graduates, and recruiting adult students to your university.

❖ SERVICE TO NONPROFIT ORGANIZATIONS

Volunteering for nonprofit organizations is a wonderful way to apply your professional talents while supporting a cause you believe in. One physical science professor with computer modeling skills began a relationship with the National Audubon Society because environmental issues were particularly important to him. Rather than just giving money or stuffing envelopes, he introduced himself to a physicist in the research department and asked what he could do. Thus began a long-term association in which the faculty member helped with a modeling project, a research project to catalog the unintended effects of renewable energy sources, and an expert system for bird identification. Professional papers were published as a result, and the professor was able to document valuable (though unpaid) experience for his resume, which enabled him to obtain research grants later in his academic career. In addition, a rewarding friendship has grown between the two scientists.

Other examples of professional service for nonprofit organizations include music professors playing in community orchestras or singing in community choruses and artists volunteering their works or services for community art exhibits or fund-raisers for art-related causes. Faculty members may also serve a valuable function by reviewing grant proposals in their area of expertise for charitable, scientific, or philanthropic funding agencies. Serving on boards of directors for nonprofit or charitable organizations is yet another way to share professional expertise.

Participating on a visitation team to evaluate other schools for reaccreditation is a valuable service as well as a learning experience that can be useful to your own institution when it comes up for reaccreditation. Faculty well-known in their fields are often asked to review the portfolios of faculty from other schools for tenure and promotion. The American Council on Education seeks professors to review nonacademic programs (such as government or corporate training programs) for possible academic credit recommendations. Science or fine arts professors may be asked to judge entries in science fairs or art contests. The possibilities are endless.

❖ REWARDS OF PROFESSIONAL SERVICE

As you have seen in the examples above, the rewards for professional service are many and varied. Figure 6.2 summarizes some of the major paybacks, both tangible and nontangible. These are organized according to the other two major roles of the faculty member, teaching and scholarship, so that the synergy of professional service with these areas is made apparent.

❖ DOCUMENTING PROFESSIONAL SERVICE

One of the sometimes unpleasant realities of academic life is the promotion and tenure process, in addition to yearly evaluations of faculty at all levels. To succeed in this often ambiguous, subjective, and political process, the faculty member must not only perform adequately in the

Benefits Related to Teaching
- Keep current in your general field
- Keep current in your area of specialization
- Develop specific case studies, exercises, and examples to use in class
- Learn new teaching techniques
- Find real-world projects for your entire class or for small groups
- Make contacts leading to internship placements for students
- Make contacts leading to job placement for your graduates
- Recruit students for your program
- Recruit adjunct faculty for your program
- Identify guest speakers for your class or department seminars
- Find interesting, real-world research projects for student independent studies, theses, and dissertations
- Discover areas where your curriculum needs to be expanded or updated
- Find people to be on your department or school's curriculum advisory council

Benefits Related to Research, Scholarship, and Creativity
- Get new ideas by interacting with people having diverse experiences
- Find real-world "laboratories" in which to try out your theories and models
- Meet collaborators outside your institution with whom you can pursue scholarly or creative work
- Discover opportunities to make professional presentations and to author or coauthor refereed and nonrefereed papers, chapters, conference proceedings, and book publications
- Find opportunities for funding
- Become better known in your field of specialization

Other Benefits
- Fulfill the professional service requirement for promotion and tenure
- Achieve self-development objectives
- Gain personal satisfaction from contributing to causes you believe in
- Establish long-term professional relationships and friendships
- Maintain a broader perspective that transcends departmental politics
- Develop paid consulting opportunities
- Feel appreciated more than you may in your academic home
- Find a new job, either inside or outside of academia, that suits you better than the one you have

Figure 6.2. Summary of Benefits From Professional Service

professional service arena but also document convincingly what has been done. William Marshall, in Chapter 5, "University Service," advocates the performance portfolio (Seldin, 1997) as an excellent way to document service. This approach encourages daily or weekly documentation of activities as they occur, resulting in an organized and impressive document at evaluation time. Diamond (1995), too, advocates the performance portfolio, as well as a faculty essay. This essay can be especially helpful in showing the linkages among professional service activities and the other faculty roles, thus presenting a coherent picture of a faculty member's contributions. For additional information on this topic, see Chapter 5.

❖ PITFALLS OF PROFESSIONAL SERVICE

The two major pitfalls of professional service are overindulgence and lack of selectivity. Faculty must be clear about their professional goals and budget their time and energy accordingly. The professional service activities you select must adequately leverage the time you have budgeted. Once people find out you are conscientious and willing to volunteer your time and professional expertise, you could find yourself constantly busy with professional service and with no time for other important activities! A full-time faculty member must keep in mind that he or she wears many hats: teacher, scholar, and provider of service to the college or university, profession, and community. A balance must be maintained among these roles.

Your particular emphasis should be determined by your own priorities and those of your college or university. If your institution values research above all else and you intend to succeed there, then professional service should take a backseat unless you can target professional service that strongly feeds your research program. Even then, you may want to emphasize the research outcomes of your activities as you prepare annual reports and promotion and tenure packets. If you work in a school that sees itself as primarily a teaching institution, then a greater amount of service will probably be expected and rewarded. But rarely does an academic institution put professional service first on its priority list. For this reason, and to keep balance in your own life, you must make sure your professional service really counts, directly or indirectly. The service you choose should meet these criteria:

- It is consistent with your teaching and scholarly interests.
- It is truly professional work—not drudgery.
- It is appreciated, or at least tolerated, by your institution.
- You enjoy the work itself.

- You learn from the experience.
- You stop when you get tired of it or it ceases to make a positive contribution to your overall goals.

❖ SUMMARY

Professional service can be the most rewarding and synergistic aspect of academic life. It can bring variety and creativity to your work, as well as a host of benefits to your students, your institution, and your profession. Carefully chosen professional service activities enhance your scholarship and your teaching, broaden your horizons, develop your skills, and bring immense personal and professional satisfaction.

❖ REFERENCES

Diamond, R. M. (1995). *Preparing for promotion and tenure review: A faculty guide*. Boston: Anker.

A faculty guide for relating public service to the promotion and tenure review process. (1993). Champaign: University of Illinois, Office of Continuing Education.

Seldin, P. (1997). *The teaching portfolio: A practical guide to improved performance and promotion/tenure decisions* (2nd ed.). Boston: Anker.

Part II

ISSUES AND TRENDS

7

Professional Development and Advancement

Rhonda J. Malone

As the old saying goes, I have some good news and some bad news. In this case they are both the same news: Today is a time of tremendous diversity and change within higher education. This diversity and change is having dramatic influences on faculty rights, roles, responsibilities, and opportunities. This chapter describes the variety, ambiguities, freedoms, constraints, and complexities that make up the state of the academic profession in contemporary American higher education. More important, it offers guidelines and suggestions for how to develop a successful and fulfilling academic career in today's higher education environment.

Twenty-five years ago, the typical new faculty member knew what was expected of him. A new assistant professor at a major research university knew he (and it was almost always he) was expected to become the best researcher possible. This meant developing a specialty within his discipline and acquiring an international reputation for scholarship. Conversely, a new faculty member at a liberal arts or comprehensive institution understood that he was expected to be an excellent teacher and provide a high quantity and quality of service to his college or university. Finally, all these new members of the professorate realized that "being a good colleague," that is, getting along well with fellow faculty members, was a crucial component of tenure attainment and future career success.

❖ CHANGING TIMES!

Today, it is quite a different story. Lack of clarity regarding responsibilities, conflicting and excessive demands, and tremendous diversity of expectations confront and confound not only new faculty but faculty at all stages of their careers. A quick review of the particularly significant changes that have occurred in recent decades includes the following.

An Expansion in the Types and Missions
of Higher Education Institutions

Although one of American higher education's trademarks has long been the diversity of its institutions, there has been an explosion in new categories of institutions. Community colleges, extension campuses, and institutions whose sole mission is the provision of distance education have all emerged in recent years. According to the Carnegie classification system, there are now 17 different categories of higher education institutions.

A Transformation in Faculty Positions

In the past, the three professorial ranks made up almost the entire faculty of most higher education institutions. Now, clinical and practitioner faculty, visiting faculty, adjunct faculty, and a cornucopia of research faculty constitute a significant part of the academic workforce. Most major research universities today have dozens of faculty titles. In addition, the number of part-time faculty has doubled in the past two decades (Schuster, 1995). By 1992, one third of faculty were part-time, and of the remaining two thirds who were full-time, 27% were in tenure-ineligible positions (Kirshtein, Matheson, Jing, & Zimbler, 1996). These trends, toward more part-time faculty and faculty in positions ineligible for tenure, are expected to continue into the foreseeable future.

Indeed, tenured members of the professorate are already a minority of the total American faculty (Lee, 1995).

Increased Criticism and Oversight of Higher Education and Its Faculty

Posttenure review, faculty workload policies, and modifications of tenure policies are all examples of attempts on the part of legislatures, state higher education agencies, and boards of trustees at increasing academic accountability. The pros and cons of tenure itself is a subject of great debate, as evidenced by articles and opinion pieces appearing in most major news publications. For example, the *Washington Post* recently included a special "Education Review" supplement (July 27, 1997) in its Sunday edition. Although the supplement included articles and book reviews on all aspects of education in America, six of the eight feature articles were editorials arguing for and against tenure. Implicit and explicit in many of the attacks on tenure are suggestions that tenure insulates a lazy, unproductive, nonresponsive faculty.

The Blurring of Institutional Missions and, Therefore, the Increased Expectations of Faculty

A phenomenon one might call "institutional creep" has been occurring during the past several decades. Two-year institutions want to expand to offer four-year degrees. Comprehensive colleges want to become research universities. Such efforts at upward mobility have resulted in expectations that faculty in these types of colleges and universities take on the additional role of published researcher. This supplementary responsibility is generally made with no decrease in teaching or service duties. Conversely, research universities are under external and internal pressure to improve the quality of their teaching. Faculty at such institutions are being told to teach more and teach better.

The Double-Edged Sword of Changing Times

One change we're all familiar with is the wondrous technological advances taking place around us. Technology has provided new and potentially improved ways to teach, to conduct research, to do literature searches, and to carry out administrative functions. A second change is the major educational paradigm shift that is taking place. This paradigm shift focuses on learning, not teaching, and outcomes, not inputs, and provides exciting new challenges. Third, the diversification of the institution's student body creates exciting cultural and academic opportunities and challenges. Another noteworthy change is the creation and advancement of different research methodologies, primarily types of qualitative research, that extend the variety of ways we can discover new knowledge. Last, calls for cross-disciplinary research and teaching efforts and pressure for improved connections between researcher and practitioner are also shaping what is expected of faculty.

Paradoxically, for each of these opportunities, there is a downside for faculty. Learning new ways of doing things while continuing to meet all one's prior roles and responsibilities puts a significant strain on the professorate. These changes require faculty to do more, often with less resources. Furthermore, it is unclear how to respond to these changes. How can one use technology to improve teaching? What curricular changes and modifications in teaching strategies are necessary to serve a changing student body and prepare them for a changing world? How does one determine quality and rigor in research that uses new methodologies or is published in new fora, such as the Internet? These questions and many more add to the challenges faculty are facing.

❖ CHANGING TIMES?

Having just presented evidence that fundamental changes are taking place within American higher education and, therefore, in the role of the professorate, let me now suggest that there are equal grounds for arguing that all this is more sound and fury than actual substance. That is to say that, although much is changing, much more is staying the same. Many of the changes that have occurred over the past decades have been at the fringes, rather than the core, of academe: either new institutions with new missions or traditional higher education institutions taking on new roles, but roles that are frequently regarded as stepchildren to the real mission of the institution. These new roles may be tolerated because of their fund-raising possibilities, because of an enthusiastic subgroup of supporters, or because it is good politics with an important constituency, but they don't represent basic changes within academe.

Thus, although there has been much public rhetoric throughout the academic community about altering paradigms and revolutionizing higher education's basic ways of viewing its mission and accomplishing that mission, many of these public proclamations are arguably unrelated to actuality. Declarations that a new day has dawned frequently appear disconnected from institutional values, rewards, infrastructures, and means of carrying out day-to-day functioning.

This is nowhere more evident than in two areas central to the faculty: first, the preparation of future faculty through doctoral education, and second, the promotion and tenure process. Robert Atwell (1996), former president of the American Council on Education, argues the first point in his final "President's Letter." He points out that doctoral education continues to produce newly minted PhDs who have been socialized to "teach in an institution where scholarship is primary and teaching loads are low" (p. 3). He even notes the symbolism that "we refer to teaching as 'load' and research as 'opportunity' " (p. 3).

Hence, new faculty enter the academic profession having been educated and inculcated into a value system that perceives the research university as the single model of institutional excellence, and the attainment of a full professorship with an international reputation as a scholar in some specialized, preferably basic, research field as the sole indication of career excellence. Atwell (1996) asserts that, despite the changing job market for academics, despite the need for faculty prepared to teach in the diverse array of the higher education institutions that exist today, despite the need for more generalized and cross-disciplinary research, despite the need to learn to incorporate new learning paradigms and to use technology in regular and distance learning education, despite all the rhetoric about dramatically changing ways in academe, our future faculty are being educated and socialized in the same manner faculty have been for decades. In other words, tomorrow's faculty are being trained to be "clones" (p. 2) of their faculty teachers and mentors who were educated in the 1950s, 60s, and 70s.

This brings me to the second point, the issue of promotion and tenure decisions. As R. Eugene Rice (1996) illustrates in *Making a Place for the New American Scholar*, during the years from approximately 1957 to 1974, "a consensus emerged regarding what it meant to be an academic professional in the fullest sense" (p. 8). These assumptions included that "research was the central professional endeavor and focus of academic life . . . the pursuit of knowledge is best organized by discipline . . . [and] professional rewards and mobility accrue to those who persistently accentuate their specializations" (p. 8). Rice emphasizes the importance of this fact by denoting that

> It is essential that we remember that the large number of older, senior faculty who now head departments and influence tenure and promotion decisions were in graduate school during those years, and this set of assumptions shaped their socialization into the profession. It is a powerful and enduring professional vision passed down and still very much alive today. (p. 9)

He contends that this results in promotion and tenure decisions based on criteria developed 30 years ago. Despite higher education's stated recognition of changing times, changing constituents, and changing needs of society, the heart and soul of attaining career success for many faculty, the determination of tenure and promotion, does not reflect this knowledge.

❖ BETWEEN A ROCK AND A HARD PLACE

What's a faculty member, particularly a new faculty member, to do? Today's professorate faces a critical lack of clarity about how to define roles. Should faculty respond to the voices that propose that change is not only necessary but already integrated into higher education's culture, values, and reward structures? What priority should be given to calls for doing things differently and calls for doing more? What risks or rewards are involved? How can faculty meet all these demands on their time and energy? What influence does all this really have on decisions such as contract renewal, tenure and promotion, and merit raises?

Not surprisingly, increased uncertainty and conflicting pressures have had negative consequences on higher education faculty. Although earlier studies of higher education faculty painted a picture of generally low stress and high satisfaction, "recent studies of academics . . . reveal dissatisfaction with work environments, disillusionment with career progress, and consequences of stress emanating from various aspects of their professional roles" (Gmelch, 1993, p. 15). For example, Melendez and de Guzman (1983) surveyed almost 2,000 faculty members at 17 colleges and found that 62% acknowledged severe or moderate job stress, and the 1995-96 Higher Education Research Institute's "The American College Teacher" faculty survey discovered that 1 in 3 faculty reported experiencing extreme stress during the past 2 years (Sax, Astin, Arrendondo, & Korn, 1996).

Of special concern is that even more difficulties are being reported during the vital early years as a faculty member. In the national study conducted by Gmelch, Wilke, and Lovrich (1986), junior faculty had statistically significant higher levels of stress than senior faculty. Dey's (1990) survey of almost 4,000 faculty also revealed higher stress levels for tenure-track faculty compared with tenured faculty on all dimensions measured. Perhaps most troubling, studies have found that stress levels of new faculty progressively increase during their first 5 years (Olsen, 1993; Sorcinelli & Gregory, 1987). This is particularly alarming given the negative consequences affecting many junior faculty's professional and personal lives. Negative effects on junior faculty's personal lives include ill health (Reynolds, 1988), fatigue, feelings of failure, marital tensions, insomnia, and anxiety attacks (Sorcinelli, 1988; Turner & Boice, 1987). Indeed, 83% of Turner and Boice's (1987) sample indicated experiencing some of the symptoms listed above.

In tenure-track faculty's professional lives, high levels of stress have been linked to decreased faculty productivity and a decline in intellectual, mental, emotional, and social performance (Gmelch, 1993; Tubesing & Tubesing, 1982). For pretenure faculty, this less-than-optimal performance can have a destructive effect on their career.

❖ THE "GOOD NEWS"

This chapter begins with a reference to the saying about good news and bad news. Those reading to this point may be waiting for the good news with baited breath. In this time, when faculty face shrinking resources, increasing ambiguity, and expanding responsibilities, just what is the positive side to the story? The answer lies in the very changes discussed. Now is a time of unprecedented possibilities. The valuing of only one model of career excellence may have been the socializing experience for many faculty, but in contemporary American higher education, there are multiple possibilities for personally and professionally fulfilling careers.

In many ways, this is an opportunity being lost. Although faculty are being besieged by difficulties, many are failing to recognize the opportunities that surround them.

To understand why this is occurring, let us examine how career planning is supposed to take place. Simplified, the career decision-making process consists of determining skills, interests, and work and personal values. This self-awareness is then used to consider various career alternatives, seeking a match of personal talents and desires with a career's characteristics, requirements, ethics, and work environment. As alluded to earlier, this has not been a process taught to or encouraged among faculty (Atwell, 1996).

A single model of career success has evolved that proposes that the most talented new doctoral graduates become employed by the most prestigious research universities possible. The best and brightest of these new faculty obtain tenure and, later, full professorship and an international reputation. Employment at any other type of institution or failure to progress up the professorial hierarchy is regarded as an indication of a second-rate academic career.

Although this prototype has by no means been universally adopted, its influence permeates American higher education. Yet its dominance fails not only those who successfully pursue it as a career path but also all those who do not. Both types of faculty are denied information about alternatives, support for considering these different options, and mentoring in how to choose and follow a path uniquely tailored to their skills, interests, and values.

❖ CAREER MANAGEMENT

What is being advocated is planned, proactive, and lifelong career management. Career management proposes a simple, but vitally different, concept that career paths should be selected and then managed to correspond with personal skills, interests, and values. It is the antithesis of the earlier proposition that there is one best academic career path, with its unstated requirement that the individual should fit into the career expectations, rather than the other way around.

Choosing and guiding one's career entails four stages.

Career Self-Awareness

Career management begins with an assessment of one's career "building blocks," that is one's personal skills, interests, and work and personal values. If asked, most faculty would probably quickly answer affirmatively to a question of whether they knew such information about themselves. Often, this is not the case, however. Faculty, like all individuals, sometimes confuse what is socially prestigious with what is personally desirable. At other times, important values are ignored or undiscovered. Skills can commonly be described in a broad sense, but not with a specificity that enables a faculty member to make informed career choices.

A quick test can ascertain an individual's career self-awareness. An effort to rank one's top five skills, interests, and values simply yet specifically can prove a surprising difficult task for many. *How to Create a Picture of Your Ideal Job or Next Career,* by Richard Bolles (1992), is an excellent guide for gaining clarity. This best-selling paperback offers a series of interesting and challenging activities to help faculty attain greater understanding of what is personally meaningful, stimulating, and challenging.

Investigation of Opportunities

Once a faculty member has a clear understanding of these career building blocks, a determination can be made about the degree to which one's current position is suitable and rewarding. Furthermore, he or she can also make a preliminary determination of future career goals. Of course, if one's present situation is a poor fit, the urgency of investigating alternatives is greater, but the importance is not. Career management requires an awareness of the opportunities available at the present time and those that could be attained in the future. Consulting or employment in industry, government agencies, research centers, or associations offers nonacademic employment options. Moving to a different type of academic institution, entering academic administration, or taking on specialized roles such as director of the department's academic advising program are options within academe. These are major changes, however.

Most career management decisions will be on a much smaller scale. Examples include a change in one's research interests or, perhaps, a cross-disciplinary approach to bring fresh perspectives to one's work. Another example is assuming a leadership role in service at the institutional, community, or disciplinary level. Still another is seeking to learn new teaching strategies, perhaps employing technology in one's teaching method, team teaching a class, or creating a new course designed for local practitioners.

Explorations of Possibilities

In determining options, another saying comes to mind: Don't jump from the frying pan into the fire. The more significant the change being considered, the more thorough an exploration of the considered change should be. Speaking with relevant people, such as individuals who have made such a career change, is one option. Sometimes a "trial run" is possible. Consulting on a part-time basis, serving as a visiting professor, or assuming an administrative role in an acting capacity all enable a faculty member to determine if a new career direction seems appropriate.

Even for smaller-scale decisions, these strategies are important. Becoming familiar with the option being considered, moving in new directions slowly, and continuing to assess whether the change being considered is, in fact, the one currently most suitable all aid in creating a rewarding, well-managed career.

Determining a Plan of Action

Many career management decisions can be easily accomplished. Others require more planning and effort. A faculty member will need to determine how to get from here to there. Professional development can play a crucial role in accomplishing many goals by providing the skills, experience, and networking contacts necessary for success.

One of the most difficult career management goals can be the most basic, finding full-time tenure-track employment. After finding out the specific disciplinary criteria needed to obtain employment at the type(s) of institutions being considered, you need a realistic plan of action for how to meet those standards and how to become acquainted and establish a reputation with helpful scholars. That's not to say that creating a plan will magically make a position appear, but failing to develop and follow through on both career planning and professional development will certainly decrease the chances of meeting one's goal.

Completing these four stages of career management is not a one-time process. Rather, it is an ongoing process, integrated into daily decisions about what actions to take, what opportunities to seek, what offers to decline, what chances not to pursue. Faculty are often envied for their autonomy. It's one of the aspects of their role that they most cherish (Sax et al., 1996). Yet they frequently act like schoolchildren who fight for their right not to have assigned classroom seats and then choose to sit in the same seat day after day.

Throughout one's career, personal and professional circumstances change. Assuming a professorship in another country for a few years may not be of interest while your children are young, but it may be a way to take on new challenge and to feel revitalized at another point in life. Using the Internet as a teaching tool for regular classroom and distance learning purposes was not available until recently. Now the chance exists to learn not only how to use this technology but also how to teach others to do so. The good news of modern times is the variety of opportunities available at every stage of one's career to develop new skills and seek new challenges.

Clearly, whether faculty members are in the early (frequently pretenure), middle, or final years of their career has a significant effect on the difficulties they confront, the opportunities and resources available to them, and the consequences that will arise from their decisions. In a moment, I will describe the four stages of the faculty career and the unique career management issues for each stage. First, however, I wish to explain the role of professional development and its centrality to career management.

❖ PROFESSIONAL DEVELOPMENT

In these rapidly changing times, there is an increasing need for continuous professional development. Faculty must acquire new skills, further develop their abilities, and remain abreast of their field. Although professional development differs as faculty move through their career, it is vital to individual faculty members, to their institution, and to the students they serve that professional development be an integral part of a faculty member's career.

Professional development incorporates a wide variety of activities. It consists of both formal programs and informal efforts. It can be either remedial or developmental (Millis, 1989). The key to useful professional development is to connect it with planned career management. The goal of developmental endeavors should be to assist in accomplishing one's current responsibilities and preparing for future responsibilities.

A plethora of programs and materials intended to provide professional development are offered today. It is important for faculty members to select activities that specifically provide the development needed at the present time. Participation in a summer 6-week multicultural curriculum transformation training program may be of interest to a tenure-track faculty member at a research university but could be unwise career management in seeking tenure. Conversely, long hours of service to disciplinary societies to the detriment of service at one's institution may be equally unwise for a liberal arts college assistant professor.

Although professional development frequently consists of organized activities, individuals often need to create their own professional development efforts. This is a crucial element of the philosophy of career management. Thus, if professional development that meet a faculty member's needs aren't available, it is the individual's responsibility to arrange his or her own development. Faculty members having difficulties with their teaching can arrange to work with a colleague whose teaching techniques they admire. A professor at a comprehensive university who wishes to pursue a career at a research university will need to create a network of advisers and mentors. This network of scholars can not only offer advice but also coauthor works, jointly seek grant funding, and provide letters of reference.

In summary, professional development is both a personal responsibility of every member of the professorate and the means by which career management can be accomplished.

❖ A DIFFICULT TASK OR A CASE OF EXCESSIVE NAIVETÉ

Many may view this with skepticism. They may accuse me of excessive naiveté, pointing to, among other things, the difficulties getting full-time academic employment, especially tenure-track positions. Furthermore, the attempt to attain tenure (or contract renewal) often creates the perception among junior faculty that they cannot manage their own careers. Instead, they believe that the need to gain approval places their future under the control of their department chair and senior faculty.

For senior faculty, the known is very reassuring. It is human nature to resist considering making significant changes in one's career. This is exemplified by the number of career counselors who remain employed in positions in which they are unhappy or unfulfilled.

These situations are realities. Career management is a difficult, at times even risky, choice. Yet there is an equally true, and risky, choice. In the rush that is the life of a faculty member today, finding the time to explore alternatives is often "put off until tomorrow" indefinitely. Many faculty denied tenure, many never-promoted associate professors, and many esteemed but unfulfilled professors never took the time to manage their career and so, instead, their careers managed them.

❖ THE FOUR STAGES OF A FACULTY CAREER

Faculty attitudes, values, focus of work efforts, concerns, skills, stress levels, and sources of satisfaction change over the course of their careers (Baldwin & Blackburn, 1981; Bowen & Schuster, 1986; Olsen, 1993; Olsen & Sorcinelli, 1992; Turner & Boice, 1989). Baldwin and Blackburn (1981) note these changes and determine that the faculty career is divided into four distinct stages. Faculty in their first 3 years of full-time experience are in the first stage, described as the novice professor. Stage 2, the early academic career, is composed of faculty who have more than 3 years experience but do not yet feel established. "The long period after one feels established but before the career disengagement process begins" (Baldwin, 1990, p. 34) constitutes the third stage: midcareer. The last phase of the academic career is stage 4: late career.

Career management varies as faculty move through their career, so a more extensive consideration of what is involved at each stage is presented here.

Stage 1: Novice Professor—Getting into the Academic World

Describing the first faculty career stage, Baldwin (1990) states that "beginning an academic career is a complex and demanding process. The new professor's major concern is competence. . . . This entry period . . . is a time of intense pressure and considerable growth" (p. 31). It is also generally a time of uncertainty about what is expected, caused in part by unclear and conflicting messages about responsibilities. New faculty often feel isolated and overwhelmed by their workload (Olsen & Sorcinelli, 1992; Tierney & Bensimmon, 1996). The following are career management and professional development issues of particular importance during these crucial early years.

Be Proactive in Learning What Is Expected

Some new faculty will find that their chair, a mentor, or a team of senior faculty members will spend considerable time providing guidance, support, and feedback about their performance. This is the exception to the rule. Most new faculty will be cheerfully greeted and then told to "shut the door and get to work!" (Eckel, MacLennan, Malone, & Riley, 1995). Although there is a tendency to follow this advice, it can lead to incorrect assumptions, inadvertent violation of local norms, and a lack of awareness of services and resources that could be vital to one's success. Therefore, despite the overwhelming workload most new faculty face, be penny wise, not pound foolish. Attend orientation programs and read policies regarding contract renewal or tenure attainment carefully. There are often institution, college, and department guidelines. Become familiar with each of them.

Figure 7.1 is a sample new faculty checklist. Tailor a similar document with specific questions and concerns and ask the department chair, or another appropriate individual, to provide this information or assign others to do so. Although there is always a chance that a chair could be irritated by such a request, it is far more likely that he or she will view the request in a positive light, perceiving the request as a sign of seriousness and dedication. It is important to remember that a new faculty member is a significant financial and time-consuming commitment on the part of the department and institution. It is in their best interest to aid junior faculty in creating a productive and successful career.

Make Connections, Form a Network, and Keep
Colleagues Informed About Your Progress

Given a heavy workload and a lack of opportunities to meet others, one of the most frustrating experiences for new faculty is often their sense of isolation. Yet making connections with others is personally and professionally important. Colleagues can be sources of information,

Providing the following information to new faculty members is beneficial to both them and the department.

_____ 1. Policies and procedures:

Long-distance phone calls	Textbook orders	Syllabi
Sick leave and collegial support	Photocopying	Course packets
Ordering supplies	Postage	Emergency numbers
List-serves for classes	Faxing	Office space
Computer support	Parking	

_____ 2. Important documents (written and electronic):

Schedule of classes	InforM	Faculty and staff directory
Academic calendar	Faculty handbook	Departmental brochure

_____ 3. Support staff assistance with preparing correspondence, ordering textbooks and supplies, making travel arrangements, maintaining files, etc.

_____ 4. Departmental communication: when and where it takes place, what is addressed, what the expectations are regarding attendance, and how to stay informed.

Department meetings	E-mail/list-serves committees
Departmental mailboxes	Program meetings

_____ 5. A departmental/college "tour" of the following areas:

Classrooms	Frequently used meeting rooms
Faculty offices	Dean's office
Rest rooms	Central offices
Where to park	Places to eat

_____ 6. Relationship with department chairperson: when there will be one-on-one meetings, what topics will be addressed, and specifically when and how it is appropriate to ask for assistance.

_____ 7. Identify and introduce contact persons for problem solving and resource questions regarding such matters as research, teaching, administrative procedures and services, and tenure review.

_____ 8. Introduce members of the department, especially those with common interests.

Figure 7.1. New Faculty Information Checklist

provide personal support, and serve as professional partners or mentors. In addition, it is critical to gaining tenure (or contract renewal) to keep colleagues abreast of one's research program and teaching skills.

Creating a network must be a conscious effort. New faculty members can attend a professional development seminar and make a few acquaintances with whom they will not have further contact. Alternatively, they can seek out individuals with whom they have some common interests, personal or academic, and exchange names and numbers to get together in the future. Similarly, it is important to plan interactions with senior faculty. For example, solicit assistance, such as guidance in developing the syllabus of a course previously taught by a senior colleague, or ask a professor with similar research interests to review a draft of a paper you are preparing for publication.

Seek Concrete, Specific Written
Feedback About Your Performance

Many new faculty do not receive an annual written evaluation of their performance. Others are given an evaluation, but the content is so general as to provide little guidance in knowing how one is progressing toward tenure (or contract renewal). What is needed is a written report containing a detailed analysis of your strengths and weaknesses in research, teaching, and service. There should be both concrete suggestions regarding areas that require improvement and a clearly stated indicator of how you are progressing toward tenure (or contract renewal). Finally, a personal meeting with the reviewer(s) will offer a chance for clarification and an exchange of ideas.

When given feedback that is ambiguous, seek clarity about what is being communicated. It can make the difference between receiving or being denied tenure (or contract renewal). Statements such as "Research seems to be of good quality but the number of publications needs to increase" can mean anything from "Continue as you are and you should have sufficient quantity by the time of your review" to "You are in DEEP trouble, and without extraordinary productivity in the next few years, you don't have a chance at tenure." If given such nebulous feedback, you should ask specific questions, such as, "Is my research productivity what you were expecting at this point in my career?" and "If I continue to produce publications at the same rate, what do you feel are my chances of attaining tenure?"

Learn How to Evaluate Information Received

As scholars, all new faculty have been educated in how to determine the rigor and quality of research in their field. Similarly, new faculty must learn to sort unsubstantiated rumor from established fact, an offhand comment from an important piece of feedback. At the same time, they must deal with conflicting advice, because they will receive just that. The source of the information, the applicability of the information to your own discipline and professional situation, and outside confirmation of the advice offered all can aid you in evaluating the multiple messages received about expectations and consequences.

Manage Your Own Career

As time passes and junior faculty gain an understanding of their role and responsibilities, as well as the culture and climate of their department and institution, it is important to assess whether there is a good fit between the individual and the position. If not, it is wiser to request a readjustment of responsibilities within the institution or to pursue employment elsewhere than to be unfulfilled and quite possibly terminated at a later date.

Stage 2: Early Academic Career—Settling Down and Making a Name

During the second stage, junior faculty "are seeking recognition and advancement" (Baldwin, 1979, p. 19). Although they are more competent, confident, and politically sophisticated, they may experience disappointment if their career has not measured up to their original expectations. Tenure-track faculty are increasingly apprehensive about their upcoming tenure evaluation. The advice offered for the first stage continues to hold true for this stage, but for faculty who are facing a formal and generally extensive review for tenure, long-term contract renewal, or job security, the following special career management suggestions apply.

The Semester Before the Formal Review Process Begins, Seek an Evaluation of the Likelihood of Success

Although no one can be a seer, chairs and senior colleagues can generally identify cases that look strong, cases that are unlikely to be successful, and the "maybe" cases in between. Consider such feedback carefully and manage your career after a thorough consideration of the options.

Clarify All Policies and Procedures
Regarding the Review Process

Written policies regarding review procedures are usually quite lengthy and often exist at the departmental, college, and institutional levels. In addition to these policies, written guidelines or seminars may be offered on how to develop a dossier. Learning this information can be critical to a successful review.

Manage Your Review Case, Including the
Development of Your Candidate Dossier

There are clearly limitations to this advice, but too few junior faculty play as active a role as they can and should in developing their own case. For example, begin in your first year developing materials documenting the strength of your teaching. Seek written peer reviews of teaching and retain letters from students that offer praise for teaching, advising, or mentorship. Also, obtain student evaluations and ensure that these evaluations are placed in some meaningful context to reviewers. For example, a 4.2 average score is useful information only if the reader is informed that this is a score on a 5-point scale and is compared with a national or departmental averages.

All tenure cases have some weaknesses. It is best to address these head-on. With teaching, for example, if teaching evaluations have been below average, provide documentation of seeking assistance and show that scores have been improving.

Finally, remember that what is considered research, teaching, and service varies by institution. Writing a textbook is an example. Be certain to develop a strong case in each of the three areas, placing stronger emphasis on whichever area has the greater importance at your particular institution.

Regardless of the Predicted or Eventual Outcome of the
Review Process, Remember to Retain Control of Your Career

Knowing that you are likely to receive tenure does not, in and of itself, determine whether you should make any significant career changes. Failure to receive tenure or contract renewal does not close all your options. The path to a new career may not be easy, but a diversity of opportunities is available and, with the appropriate efforts, obtainable.

Stage 3: Midcareer—Accepting a Career Plateau or Setting New Goals

By far the longest of the career stages, the third stage begins after one feels established in one's profession and lasts until "career disengagement" begins.

> This is often a very productive and rewarding phase, a time when professors enjoy maximum professional influence. . . . For many, it is also a transitional phase. Interests and concerns that were dormant during the intense early-career years may bubble to the surface. . . . Frequently, midcareer parallels the onset of a career plateau. After many years in the classroom or laboratory, a professor may begin to note a monotonous sameness about his or her work. A fear that professional challenges and growth have ended may develop. . . . Additionally, the professor who has reached a plateau lacks the concrete goals, and clear sense of direction, that make the early career so exciting. (Baldwin, 1990, p. 34)

Professional development and career management play a fundamental role in determining the degree of satisfaction, animation, and fulfillment you will feel during midcareer.

Be Prepared for Difficult Transitions After Promotions

Most faculty seeking tenure and promotion to associate professor, and later promotion to (full) professor, fail to realize that, despite the joy, relief, and sense of accomplishment that comes with these successes are difficulties. Faculty often initially feel directionless. Having achieved the goal they were so adamantly pursuing, they are left feeling uncertain about what to pursue next. In addition, faculty also may have a sense of being an "impostor." Having joined the ranks of their more senior colleagues, they may be plagued with a sense that they don't fit in. This is a normal part of all transitions, even positive ones. You have to let go of a former identity and allow time to acquire a view of yourself in a new role. Just knowing that it is a normal experience should ease the adjustment.

Keep Your Options Open

The best way to avoid a plateau is to never reach it, and the best way to accomplish that is to assess your skills, interests, and values continually and explore options that enable you to be constantly challenged and excited by your work. Avoiding burnout, alienation, and a sense of career failure requires proactive effort throughout the midcareer stage.

Stage 4: Late Career—Leaving a Legacy

This stage consists of "the years before retirement, when gradual disengagement from work ordinarily occurs" (Baldwin, 1990, p. 36). Unlike years past, when retirement at the age of 70 was often required and when few opportunities to remain actively involved in academe existed, a faculty member entering the later years of his or her career today has an assortment of opportunities available. A partial listing includes serving as a part-time faculty member at your own or a new institution, involvement in community service using disciplinary expertise, becoming a consultant, and retiring to a life that includes an active intellectual life, such as participating in Elderhostels or moving to retirement communities especially designed for scholars. Thus, even when a career as it has been historically defined is ended, career management and professional development help create a rewarding and stimulating intellectual and personal life.

❖ REFERENCES

Atwell, R. (1996, August 30). *President's letter.* Washington, DC: American Council on Education.

Baldwin, R. G. (1979). *Faculty career development* (Current Issues in Higher Education No. 2). Washington, DC: ASHE-ERIC.

Baldwin, R. G. (1990). Faculty career stages and implications for professional development. In J. H. Schuster, D. W. Wheeler, & Associates (Eds.), *Enhancing faculty careers: Strategies for development and renewal* (pp. 20-40). San Francisco: Jossey-Bass.

Baldwin, R. G., & Blackburn, R. T. (1981). The academic career as a developmental process. *Journal of Higher Education, 52*(6), 598-614.

Bolles, R. (1992). *How to create a picture of your ideal job or next career.* Berkeley: Ten Speed.

Bowen, H. R., & Schuster, J. H. (1986). *American professors: A national resource imperiled.* New York: Oxford University Press.

Dey, E. L. (1996). *Dimensions of faculty stress: Evidence from a recent national survey.* Washington, DC: ASHE-ERIC.

Eckel, P., MacLennan, R. Malone, R., & Riley, D. (1995). *The UMCP junior faculty experience.* Unpublished manuscript.

Education review. (1997, July 27). *Washington Post.*

Gmelch, W. H. (1993). *Coping with faculty stress.* Newbury Park, CA: Sage.

Gmelch, W. H., Wilke, P. K., & Lovrich, N. P. (1986). Dimensions of stress among university faculty: Factor-analysis results from a national study. *Research in Higher Education, 24,* 266-286.

Kirshstein, R. J., Matheson, N., Jing, Z., and Zimbler, L. J. (1996). *Institutional policies and practices regarding faculty in higher education.* Washington, DC: Department of Education, Office of Educational Research and Improvement, National Center for Education Statistics.

Lee, J. (1995, September). *National Education Association update: Tenure.* Washington, DC: National Education Research Center.

Melendez, W. A., & de Guzman, R. M. (1983). *Burnout: The new academic disease* (ASHE-ERIC Higher Education Research Report No. 9). Washington, DC: ASHE-ERIC.

Millis, B. (1989). Faculty development: An imperative for the 1990's. *MAHE Journal, 15,* 9-21.

Olsen, D., & Sorcinelli, M. D. (1992). The pre-tenure years: A longitudinal perspective. In M. D. Sorcinelli & A. E. Austin (Eds.), *Developing new and junior faculty* (pp. 15-26). San Francisco: Jossey-Bass.

Olsen, D. (1993). Work satisfaction and stress in the first and third year of academic appointment. *Journal of Higher Education, 64,* 453-471.

Reynolds, A. (1988). *Making and giving the grade: Experiences of beginning professors at a research university.* Paper presented at the annual meeting of the American Educational Research Association, New Orleans, LA.

Rice, R. E. (1996). *Making a place for the new American scholar.* Washington, DC: American Association for Higher Education.

Sax, L. J., Astin, A. W., Arrendondo, M., & Korn, W. S. (1996). *The American college teacher: National norms for the 1995-96 HERI faculty survey.* Los Angeles: Higher Education Research Institute.

Schuster, J. H. (1995, Fall). Wither the faculty? The changing academic labor market. *Educational Record,* 28-33.

Sorcinelli, M. D. (1988). Satisfactions and concerns of new university teachers. In J. Kurfiss, L. Hilsen, S. Kahn, M. D. Sorcinelli, &. R. Tiberius (Eds.), *To improve the academy: Resources for students, faculty, and institutional development* (Vol. 7, pp. 121-134). Stillwater, OK: POD/New Forum.

Sorcinelli, M. D., & Gregory, M. W. (1987). Faculty stress: The tension between career demands and "having it all." In *Coping with faculty stress* (Vol. 29, pp. 43-52). San Francisco: Jossey-Bass.

Tierney, W. G., & Bensimmon, E. M. (1996). *Community and socialization in academe.* Albany: State University of New York Press.

Tubesing, N. L., & Tubesing, D. A. (1982). The treatment of choice: Selecting stress skills to suit the individual and the situation. In W. S. Paine (Ed.), *Job stress and burnout: Research, theory, and intervention perspectives* (pp. 155-171). Newbury Park, CA: Sage.

Turner, J. L., & Boice, R. (1987). Starting at the beginning: The concerns and needs of new faculty. In J. Kurfiss, L. Hilsen, S. Kahn, M. D. Sorcinelli, & R. Tiberius (Eds.), *To improve the academy: Resources for students, faculty, and institutional development* (Vol. 7, pp. 41-55). Stillwater, OK: POD/New Forum.

❖ SUGGESTED READINGS

Frost, P., & Taylor, M. S. (Eds.). (1996). *Rhythms of academic life*. Newbury Park, CA: Sage. This is an excellent series of articles that discuss almost every aspect and option of an academic's career. Written by business and management faculty, their experiences and advice are generally useful to all faculty.

Whicker, M., Kronenfeld, J. J., & Strickland, R. (1993). *Getting tenure*. Newbury Park, CA: Sage. Although this book takes a somewhat extreme view of how politicized the tenure review process is, it offers a great deal of useful advice for tenure-track faculty.

8

New Learning Approaches
Conceptualizing the
Learning-Teaching Interaction

Sharon Johnson Confessore

This chapter discusses a new way of thinking about the teaching-learning interaction. As college and university students become more diverse and technology becomes an integral part of the teaching process, the ways learners and teachers interact will change. This chapter presents hypotheses about the effects of the changing college experience and provides some suggestions for faculty to consider as they adjust to this new teaching situation.

❖ CHARACTERISTICS OF THE NEW
COLLEGE AND UNIVERSITY ENVIRONMENT

In the late 1990s, the university has begun to change from a place that educates young people and prepares them for life to a learning center that people of all ages use to help them respond to changes in their lives.

165

They come seeking assistance in changing careers and to revitalize themselves and increase their knowledge. The knowledge revolution and accompanying technological advancements, demographic changes that redefine the typical college student, and the importance of lifelong learning have contributed to reconceptualizing how we think about the role and purpose of a college and, as a result, the college professor. The university is changing from a purveyor of information to a developer and supporter of lifelong learners.

These changes will have profound implications for the teaching-learning interaction. Personal computers and the Internet have already made it possible for learners to "connect" to virtual universities, never enter a library, and communicate with faculty members at any time and wherever they find themselves. Compared to the typical college student of only a few years ago, today's student is older and more likely to be managing multiple life responsibilities, such as parent, caregiver, and spouse. The average length of time to finish college has increased from 4 to 7 years, largely because the relationship between work and college studies has been reversed for many students. College traditionally was seen as a stepping stone to a career, and work was undertaken as a secondary activity intended to defray college costs and to provide experience.

Today, students are more likely to be fully employed and to view college studies as a means to change careers or obtain a promotion. In addition, more students come to college with significant life experience. Many of this new breed of student want "just in time" learning to enhance their employment status and competence on the job. They must be able to see the practical applications of learning to the demands of their life circumstances. These changes present challenges to the college teacher who is working with individuals who come to the teaching-learning interaction with multiple motives and needs. To have their individual learning needs met, students must become "responsible learners," able to manage their own learning experience.

In addition to changes in the life circumstances and motivations of students, colleges are faced with a rapidly changing and expanding knowledge base. The knowledge revolution necessitates continuous learning throughout the life span, requiring new learning capabilities. The ability to identify resources and analyze and evaluate information is critical in a world where information is available on demand. Individuals develop very complex and sophisticated ways of accessing information, yet this is tempered by the individual's own well-established beliefs about learning efficacy and established learning habits. For students to become competent, they must develop strategies that ensure an open mind to new solutions and alternatives, and a capacity to seek out, make sense of, and assign value to widely disparate information.

These conditions change the way we think about colleges and college teaching. In an environment where there are no classrooms, how do we define a class? If we acknowledge that each person has unique learning needs, how do we determine what should be taught? If the half-life of knowledge continues to decrease, how do we ever establish a body of knowledge that is stable and immutable? All these conditions require that the college shift from teaching students to developing learners. College faculty of the future will not "profess," they will empower through learning. Classes will become obsolete and be replaced by learning interactions. These may occur virtually and involve only those individuals who need or can contribute to the knowledge being exchanged. These events will be designed and initiated by the learners. A professor may be seen as the individual who organizes these events, but in a world where so much information is so easily accessible, the notion that one individual has the responsibility to tell students what they need to know will be viewed as nonsense.

The way we conceptualize learning will be altered. This change will be driven by two fundamental changes within colleges. First, learning will be considered a continuous and integral part of the life-development process, and technology will make this idea a reality. Second, colleges will no longer be place bound, and students will not be dependent on the knowledge base of the instructor or the contents of the library. In this new college, students will be able to access information independently and efficiently, using multiple resources, most of them electronic. The ability to learn through self-planned learning interactions will become critical in the future.

The remainder of this chapter is designed to help faculty bridge these next years. It presents hypotheses about the effects of the changing college experience and provides some suggestions for faculty to consider as they adjust to this new teaching arena.

❖ THE FACULTY-STUDENT RELATIONSHIP

In the future, the emphasis on formalized educational experiences will diminish in favor of highly individualized, custom-designed, self-initiated learning events. In essence, "students" will become "learners." This means that they will take control of the planning, initiating, and carrying out of their learning experiences. Learners will devise learning projects, which will account for learning need, current level of knowledge, and knowledge acquisition preferences. This will require that the new students be autonomous learners. These self-directed learners will possess four critical capabilities. They will have a desire to learn; have the initiative to undertake a learning project; be resourceful in obtaining the learning support needed; and have the persistence to continue the project to its completion (Candy, 1991).

The faculty member of the future will need to have the skills and temperament necessary to support the learners as they develop or refine these capabilities. In the college of the future, the faculty role will expand from establishing the purpose of a course and delivering instruction, to helping learners organize their learning program over a lifetime. Faculty and learners will work together to identify the best program for each individual, which will be revised regularly throughout the individual's life. Consideration will be given to meeting both short- and long-term learning needs and devising a scheme for the individual that matches life and career needs. For example, individuals who need new skills to meet work demands may require a series of "courses" downloaded over the computer, whereas an individual just starting out in the work world may require a series of meetings with various experts in several related fields. For individuals who are interested in child development, sessions with other caregivers can be organized, whereas for those concerned about the aging process, opportunities to frame their lives in context would be appropriate.

These interactions may be held virtually or they may be held on-site as part of a seminar series. They might even be held without the "teacher" present. The distinguishing characteristic of all these scenarios is that each will be unique, designed by the learner in consultation with a faculty member after careful consideration of the learner's circumstances, needs, and existing knowledge base. Further, these interactions will provide the learner with an opportunity to enhance his or her desire to learn and provide the impetus to undertake a learning project.

Another role for the faculty member will be to help learners identify resources and understand their reasons for undertaking a learning project, making it possible to frame learning goals and take a project to completion. This role is critical to ensuring that the learner is able to access appropriate resources and devise a learning project that is relevant and meaningful. In supporting learners as they assess and diagnose their learning needs, the faculty member takes the role of mentor—simultaneously helping the learner frame the learning need while providing a reality check of the learner's capabilities and limitations. For learners who are inexperienced in assessing their own capabilities, the faculty member's role will become one of helping to attribute success and failure (not an easy task for some students, who tend to take either all the credit or all the blame). Faculty will also help learners objectively identify barriers and enhancers to their learning. These processes will organize the learning process so that it is productive.

❖ TAKING RESPONSIBILITY FOR LEARNING

The students of the future will be independent learners who take responsibility for their own learning. By virtue of computers and the information highway, students will enter college better prepared to access and use information. The consumer mentality of current students, that faculty are there to dispense information, will be altered by the students' prior experiences and use of the technology. The faculty member of the future will play a key role in ensuring that this change takes place, however, for although students will enter the college arena much better prepared and ready to be autonomous learners, they will need to learn how to accomplish several different goals. These include developing standards and criteria for their own performances, the ability to explain phenomena in various circumstances, and the capacity to form opinions and clarify beliefs independently. A critical capability will be the capacity to construct meaning and assign value to information.

These goals, currently ideals to be pursued, will become even more important in the future. They make it possible for the learner to take information and organize it into meaningful data. By being able to determine a standard of excellence for themselves, learners will structure their knowledge-gathering activities to ensure that complete information is being analyzed. College faculty will be key players in this process. They will serve as consultants, helping students balance the process of establishing boundaries with the information gathering so that the analysis phase can begin, while simultaneously pushing students forward, ensuring that full consideration is given to all appropriate information.

Today, information is presented within the context of the class in which it is taught, and much effort is made to provide practical experiences to ensure that students know how to apply the seemingly disconnected knowledge. For students of the future, obtaining information in virtual learning situations will be easy. In the future, learning will, in large part, occur at an individual's place of work and will be intimately tied to the need for job-related knowledge. The challenge for both students and faculty will be to ensure that the information obtained goes beyond just the practical. Faculty members will need to encourage learners to study phenomena across varied situations, seeking out knowledge and sources that might, at first inspection, not directly relate to the topic at hand. Faculty in the future may need to help learners identify broad areas of study and knowledge that expand their understanding of the world and help learners think creatively.

One of the biggest challenges facing the faculty member of the future will be coaching learners to develop the capacity to form opinions independently and clarify beliefs. Of all the goals necessary for independent learners, this is the most important. Information, no matter how accessible, is useless—and perhaps even dangerous—without the sagacity to understand one's own belief structure and the capacity to develop well-formed and substantiated opinions. These are clearly necessary skills for current students. In classrooms where lecture method and one-way transmission of information prevail, however, these capacities are not developed. Faculty of the future, released from the task of simply transmitting information, will instead become responsible for ensuring that students are able to manage information. They will be valued for their ability to develop the capacity for independent thinking, careful analysis, and creative problem solving.

❖ SUPPORTING MEANING DEVELOPMENT

In a society where the amount of information will increase at a phenomenal rate and access to it will be unlimited, a key role of the faculty member is to help the individual make meaning and assign value to information. It is possible, for example, for learners to speak directly to researchers and theoreticians via e-mail. This means the role of faculty member as disseminator of information is obsolete, for the student can now obtain information by himself or herself. The teacher's role will become one of helping learners frame information and construct new meaning schemes.

Mezirow (1994) describes this process as *communicative learning*. Communicative learning involves trying to understand what someone means. This type of learning is contrasted with *instrumental learning*, which is learning how to control or manipulate the environment. Instrumental learning relies on identifying learning needs and tasks, behavioral objectives, and measurable learning gains. These components of education, although important, will share emphasis with communicative learning techniques. These include the capacity to reflect critically on developing insights, validate beliefs, and transform information into meaning schemes. The faculty member of the future will spend much less time communicating information and much more time helping students develop their meaning schemes. The faculty member's role will become one of helping individuals develop the capacity to reason and participate fully and equally in discourse, and thus develop new insights and meanings of the world.

It could be argued (and is, among liberal arts faculty) that this has always been the primary task of the college faculty member. The importance of developing this ability will be paramount in the future, however, and will be necessary even in the "career preparation" majors, such as business and education. Changing the emphasis of learning in college to one of reflection and making meaning will fundamentally alter what the college faculty member does. Faculty members of the future will provide opportunities and vehicles for this reflective process. They will help students weigh arguments and determine the efficacy of alternatives. Finally, the faculty member will provide means by which learners will be able to use the masses of information they access individually and autonomously.

❖ COLLEGES' ROLE AND THEIR EFFECT ON LEARNING

The role of colleges will be perceived very differently in the future. This will frame the purposes and missions of these institutions and affect how the teaching-learning interaction occurs. A large amount of learning and teaching is already occurring in business and industry, and the increasing number of corporate universities is instructive. The amounts of money being spent by corporations on their own educational systems and their influence in universities caused by tuition-paid programs suggest even more extensive influence and replacement of traditional college roles.

This specific trend in business is supported by the trend toward viewing learning as a lifelong process. Increasingly, individuals are looking to colleges to provide opportunities for learning in all its contexts, including recreation. Increasingly, learning is being seen as integral to living. Within this context, colleges become more than just a place to get a degree; they become the community center of the future—the place where experts are available to enhance the natural process of learning.

Today, students can earn their degrees without ever attending a class session on a college campus. Increasingly, colleges are relying on off-site facilities, teaching classes in offices, companies, and specially constructed buildings, placed strategically within the areas where people live and work so that classes are convenient and accessible. In the future, students will never have to leave their homes or places of work to obtain their degrees. Further, because of the increasing importance of obtaining new knowledge, the idea of regularly scheduled classes taking place on a campus will become obsolete, primarily because individuals will require and be able to access information immediately.

Understanding why individuals engage in the learning process will be key in these new colleges. Individuals tend to engage in the learning process for one of three reasons: for social purposes (they are motivated by the interaction with others); for goal-oriented purposes (they have an external reason for acquiring this particular knowledge); and for learning reasons (they enjoy learning new things) (Houle, 1961). Each of these purposes determines, in large part, why learners engage the learning process and how they will proceed through the experience. It also makes it possible for faculty members to help learners match learning activities and events with individual needs. For the classroom of the future, for example, faculty members, using these categories, will be able to determine which students will benefit from on-line interaction when others need face-to-face instruction. This framework will allow the faculty member to help the learner select the best medium for instruction, maximizing the learning opportunity. By helping students clarify their learning goals, college faculty will help learners identify the best strategies and means for acquiring information. Students who are goal oriented are most likely to engage in the learning process when they need information to answer a specific question, probably related to their job or a specific life issue. Faculty of the future will work with these students to identify learning projects designed to address the immediate need, with little regard for where the learning event occurs.

Future faculty duties will include helping learners design events that incorporate and ensure interaction for students who are social learners. With the increasing capacity of technology, this does not necessarily mean face-to-face events. Ensuring productive and effective interaction will be an increasingly important part of a faculty member's role, however. Given the range of potential learning situations, faculty members of the future may become intellectual matchmakers, helping learners identify colleagues who have similar interests and learning needs. Faculty might also serve as learning team leaders, helping groups frame a learning problem, identifying areas of study and sources of information, and negotiating as the group determines its means of assessment.

Learning for the sake of learning is increasingly popular in the United States. People are viewing learning as a recreational activity. Programs such as Elderhostel and continuing education courses deliver instruction in everything from studying opera to classical French cooking. Colleges are devoting more resources to individuals who simply enjoy learning new things. With the redefinition of work and the increasing life span expectancy, these programs will expand college course offerings.

This emphasis provides new opportunities for faculty of the future. Faculty will find themselves in demand as learning event organizers—individuals who identify interesting and exciting nontraditional topics and opportunities for learning. New ways of thinking about how to package and market information so that it is viewed as entertainment will become necessary. Successful colleges of the future will rely on faculty who understand that helping learning-oriented students meet their educational goals means viewing teaching as a process of stimulating students' basic need to know. These students will conduct their own learning projects but will rely on the faculty member to serve as guide and framer of interesting topics.

All three of these learning types provide new ways of framing learning in the future. By understanding the motivations for engaging in learning, faculty will be better able to understand the learner's goals. This will make it possible for faculty to help students access the information they desire using the means that is most appropriate.

❖ WHAT IS THE NEW LEARNING?

When considering learning in the future, one must also consider the role of teaching in the future, for both will be fundamentally altered. The future of learning requires an entirely different way of thinking about faculty roles. College students of the future will rely on three key abilities: (1) the ability to access information independently and efficiently; (2) the ability to manage their own learning experiences and become responsible learners; and (3) the ability to assign value to widely disparate information. Each of these abilities will require the support of a learning coach, one who is capable of helping learners identify learning needs and motivations. It may be possible that, in the future, selected faculty members will become "franchise teachers," individuals who are in such demand for their prowess in stimulating learning that everyone wants to undertake a learning project under their guidance. These super-coaches will guide learners as they make meaning of experiences, new knowledge, and interactions with others. They will help learners as they create new knowledge as well as determine the efficacy of existing information.

In the final analysis, "new" learning approaches may be a misstatement, because techniques currently available, particularly within the self-directed and adult learning literature, provide a means for understanding the future of learning. The future of learning is distinguished by the fact that the learner will explicitly control the time, place, and content of interaction. The faculty member will be more explicitly a coach and mentor who helps learners access information independently and efficiently, manage their own learning experiences, and assign value to widely disparate information. Most important, this individual will help develop open and creative minds, a task surprisingly similar and no less challenging than it is today.

❖ REFERENCES

Candy, P. (1991). *Self-direction for lifelong learning*. San Francisco: Jossey-Bass.

Houle, C. O. (1961). *The inquiring mind* (2nd ed.). Norman: University of Oklahoma, School of Education, Oklahoma Research Center for Continuing Professional and Higher Education.

Mezirow, J. (1994). Understanding transformation theory. *Adult Education Quarterly, 44*, 222-235.

9

Technology

Computers, Distance Learning, and the Virtual University

Theodore E. Stone

Technology is expanding students' ability to have greater access to resources at school, at home, and at work. This trend is coinciding with shifting trends in higher education toward total quality commitment and customer-oriented education. Faculty members who are newly hired will be increasingly expected to develop and electronically publish on-line resources to support expanding distance education programs at home, in the workplace, and at satellite campuses.

Consider the following case scenarios.

Scenario A

Professor Jones has just been hired by Enormous State University to teach in the history department. His department chair has encouraged him to use a class e-mail list to improve how the students in the class communicate and collaborate together. The department chair encourages Professor Jones to send out an electronic question of the week over the e-mail list to the students in the class. Imagine Professor Jones's surprise when he logs into his e-mail account the next day to find more than 120 messages waiting for him. "Am I expected to respond to all these?" he thinks to himself as he prepares for an unexpectedly very long day on campus.

Scenario B

Dr. Smith's new faculty appointment promises to be an exciting one. She has been asked by her department chair to develop a new English literature course for nonnative speakers of English. The course will be delivered over the Web over compressed two-way video conferencing. Through meeting colleagues at conferences and over the Internet, she has discovered that there may be 15 students in Cali, Colombia, who would like to participate in the course next semester. The dean insists that these students pay out-of-state tuition, however. The students decline to enroll because the out-of-state tuition rates are too high. In the meantime, Dr. Smith hears that the university from a neighboring state has just begun offering a distance learning course in her community, and it is offering a tuition that is even less than her school's tuition.

These two scenarios illustrate some of the problems and dilemmas facing faculty as they begin to implement technology into the curriculum. In the first case, Professor Jones was surprised to find out how much work he had created for himself when he created an e-mail class list; at that point, he still hadn't discovered if e-mail could really improve how his students learned. In the second scenario, Dr. Smith had developed a new on-line course and had even begun to recruit students, but she was caught in her university's tuition policies, which seem out of step with the realities of the electronic age.

These two instructors are confronting some of the very real dilemmas of teaching with technology. Teaching with technology holds the promise not only of improving the quality of how students learn but of facilitating when and where they learn. The sands have shifted. Now faculty members may expect that the traditional paradigm will hold: Students come to the university on the university's schedule. In this traditional view of higher education, the professor teaches in the classroom, in which students attentively listen and take notes and are thus transformed.

The new paradigm for higher education is based on attentiveness to the customer. In this case, the student is the customer. In a reversal of the old orders, the university is expected to go to the student, not the other way around. This means that the university must be able to provide a virtual education on demand, delivering education wherever the student is located and whenever he or she is ready for it. For example, if a university is offering advanced degrees in health care or nuclear engineering, the university had better be prepared to give potential students full access to the course, even if the students are working the night shift at the hospital or the power plant.

This chapter explores some of the issues related to the incorporation of technology into curriculum. The first section examines some theories of how technology may affect how people learn. The second section examines how technology can be used to engage students and to connect them to one another. Some of the technology examined in this chapter includes tools such as e-mail, the World Wide Web (WWW, the Web), two-way interactive compressed video, and one-way satellite television. The third section explores some of the issues involving course material and intellectual property rights. Topics in this section include concerns about losing control of material on the WWW, design and development of course materials, and developing course-specific CD-ROMs. The fourth section explores issues around faculty workload. This section focuses on time requirements for developing new materials, the effort required for delivery of electronic courses, faculty compensation, and faculty recognition for promotion and tenure.

❖ OVERVIEW OF MEDIATED INSTRUCTION

Behaviorist Perspective

Notions of how people learn through computer-mediated instruction have shifted substantially over the past 30 years. This shift reflects, if nothing else, general notions of how people acquire knowledge. Thirty years ago, the dominant theory of learning was behaviorism. In this theory of knowledge acquisition, there is *stimulus* and there is *response*. There is not much else. There is no thought, per se. To the pure behaviorist, thought is merely a very complex series of stimuli and responses.

The behaviorist view of learning gained popularity in the early part of this century as a more scientifically testable position than some other views of learning (such as exercising mental faculties or humanistic theories of development). Behaviorists define learning as changes in behavior or, more precisely, a change in the learner's capacity to behave in novel ways not brought about by mere maturation or growth. It follows that changes in behavior are brought about by influences in the environment. Environmental stimuli bring increasingly complex responses. Therefore, complex learning is the gradual building up of larger and more complex patterns of stimulus and response (Romiszowski, 1986). Early supporters of this theory of knowledge acquisition include Thorndike, Pavlov, and B. F. Skinner.

It should come as a surprise that Skinner (1986) was an enthusiast of technology-mediated instruction. Using a technique he called "programmed instruction," Skinner experimented with teaching machines: contraptions that provided stimuli in the form of information for learners to read and to respond to, providing rewards for correct responses. By the mid-1980s, Skinner had expressed great enthusiasm for the personal computer. In fact, he viewed computers as the natural extension of his work in programmed instruction. Skinner even said that microcomputers were the most powerful, efficient teaching machines.

Skinner (1986) felt that his view explained learners' motivation and attention when learning via microcomputers. This interaction of learner and machine might also be explained as the *Nintendo effect*. One does not need to observe children playing video games very long to observe that there is an inherent interaction between the learner and the machine that stimulates motivation. That is, because of the constant stream of rewards for correct or appropriate responses, the nature of the computer itself provides stimulus and response to encourage additional interaction. Although this view may explain computer-based learning that involves declarative knowledge (where it is easy to reward a simple correct answer), it does not explain how people acquire more complex knowledge, such as problem-solving skills or critical thinking skills.

Cognitivist Perspective

Much of the computer-based learning developed in the 1960s and 1970s reflected the programmed instruction approach to learning. In the 1980s, a shift began to occur from a behaviorist approach in learning to a cognitive psychology perspective in learning. The principal difference between this model and the behaviorist model is that learning is more than just stimulus and response. Cognitive psychologists argue that an individual processes a stimulus—thinks about it—and then responds. Cognitivists believe that there is such a phenomenon as thought. They tend to think in terms of learners developing schema or a *gestalt* of a subject. The way computers are used to aid learning from this perspective is very different from the behaviorist perspective.

Two cognitivist theories are now predominant with regard to computer-based instruction: social learning theory and constructionism. Both theories give rise to the view of *computer-mediated* instruction instead of *computer-based* or *computer-aided* instruction.

Proponents of social learning theory suggest that humans are inherently social animals. By and large they live together, work together, and learn together. Social interaction is an inherent aspect of how people acquire knowledge. Albert Bandura (1977), a proponent of this theory, writes that "in the social learning view, people are neither driven by innate forces nor buffeted by environmental stimuli. Rather, psychological functioning is explained by a continuous reciprocal interaction of personal and environmental determinants." From this point of view, anything that enhances a person's ability to interact with his or her environment, particularly with regard to a topic of study, can enhance learning.

Here is an example.

A student at a bakery has a new idea: He can sell more bread if it is sliced first. (The greatest idea since sliced bread!) Through social interaction and through interaction in the environment, the student can begin to test this idea. The student may ask customers if they like the idea of sliced bread. The student may ask the opinion of the master baker or other students at the bakery. The student might even observe other bakeries. Through this type of interaction, the student is able to think critically and problem solve creatively with regard to his subject.

Using computers and technology to support this type of learning would be markedly different from using computers for Skinner's (1986) programmed instruction. Programmed instruction would require that the instruction be linear, advancing the learner step by step, building complex responses on top of simpler responses through controlled stimuli. Computer instruction that supports the social learning approach would be inherently nonlinear. Students would hyperlink to resources based on intuition and curiosity. In addition, computers would be used for communication to other students, to instructors, and to experts. The hyperlinking nature of the WWW is supportive of this approach to computer-based instruction.

Constructivist learning theory is linked to social learning theory. Constructivism suggests that meaning is intimately connected with experience (Hanley, 1994). The learner will understand new information only if it is connected to knowledge already in memory. The role of the teacher is to organize information around conceptual clusters of problems and to engage student interest. Teaching from a constructivist approach would customary follow some sort of inquiry method (Dettrick, n.d.). This suggests that there is a primary hands-on, problem-centered approach, with the focus on learning and applying appropriate investigational and analytical strategies.

The WWW, e-mail, and video conferencing all open up to the student a gateway to the world. Computer-centered instruction is no longer a self-contained module. Instead, it becomes a central resource for the student's intellectual inquiries.

Shneiderman (1993) describes his philosophy about this as "construction and engagement." He writes that at the classroom level, students are engaged with each other constructing meaningful products of substance. Shneiderman believes that computers and computer-based communication technology have empowered students—and instructors—in remarkable ways. He believes these technologies make for a truly interactive learning environment.

Transactional Distance

Many university instructors may scoff at the notion of taking or teaching a correspondence course. The very idea invokes in many people the image of the advertisements inside matchbook covers inviting readers to test out their talent at the Great Artists Correspondence School. For many people living in remote and isolated areas of the world, however, correspondence courses are the most practical way to earn a college degree or to advance professionally. Historically, correspondence schools shipped to students textbooks, learning materials, modules, and syllabi for the course. Frequently, these programs would be "open"; that is, there would be no fixed deadlines for completion of the material—the course would be completed when the correspondence student finished the work.

Over time, correspondence schools began to include audiotapes and telephone communication with students. In the 1960s and 1970s, short-wave broadcasts were used for lectures in certain parts of the world. It was at this time that researchers in distance learning began to notice a phenomenon with regard to distance education students. Distance for students was transactional rather than physical. This is to say, students who attended a lecture all semester with 500 other students but who never spoke with the professor could be transactionally more distant from the instructor than a student who was 500 miles away from campus but spoke with the instructor once each week by telephone. Likewise, distance education students who collaborate on a group project together via e-mail and the WWW could be transactionally closer to each other than students at a lecture hall who never meet outside class.

Interactivity and collaboration are the most important aspects of the contemporary use of computers in instruction. This emphasis on interactivity and collaboration reflects the migration of computers in education from being mere Skinnerian teaching machines to gateways to resources and people to support the creation of new and meaningful knowledge.

The next section focuses on some of the current tools in use to support the connectivity of students to the instructor, to one another, and to the world.

❖ CONNECTIVITY TOOLS AND STUDENT ENGAGEMENT

A spectrum of techniques, tools, and technologies is available to the university instructor to enhance teaching in a face-to-face environment as well as at a distance. Although the following list is far from exhaustive, it reflects some of the techniques currently in use at many colleges and universities. This section explores the following technology options for teaching:

- Satellite and one-way transmission of educational television
- Two-way or multiway compressed video teleconferencing
- E-mail and the use of electronic mailing lists and list-serves
- WWW and on-line course resources
- CU-SeeMe and real-time video conferencing over the Internet

Satellite and One-Way Educational Television

One-way educational television continues to be used throughout the United States in many forms. Although it has its critics, it remains an effective means of delivering lectures to distance learners throughout a region. One-way television can be delivered via satellite, microwave transmissions (both live broadcast and previously recorded broadcast), cable television, or videotapes. The advantage of participating in a live broadcast is the ability to interact with the instructor, albeit in a limited way, via telephone or fax. The advantage of a previously recorded lecture is that a student can watch the lecture on his or her own schedule.

The state of Utah delivers instructional television via the Educational Network of Utah. In a survey of student attitudes there, researchers compared three modes of instruction: conventional face-to-face teaching, live broadcasting of lectures, and videotapes of lectures viewed in small groups with a facilitator (Egan, Welch, Page, & Sebastian, 1992). They found that students preferred the face-to-face meetings in these three scenarios, mostly because of intimacy issues—being able to access and respond immediately to the instructor.

The intimacy issue is also a problem for the instructor. Teaching face-to-face provides the instructor with a host of visual feedback, for example, students looking puzzled or fidgeting in their chairs. Professors do not get that sort of feedback by maintaining eye contact with a camera lens.

The University of Idaho's College of Engineering provides a set of recommendations for instructors who are preparing to teach on instructional television. These are provided in Figure 9.1.

- Before developing something new, check and review existing materials for content and presentation ideas.
- Analyze and understand the strengths and weaknesses of the possible delivery systems available (e.g., audio, video, data, print) not only in terms of how they are delivered (e.g., satellite, microwave, fiber optic cable), but in terms of learner needs and course requirements before selecting a mix of instructional technology.
- Hands-on training with the technology of delivery is critical for both teacher and students. Consider a preclass session in which the class meets informally using the delivery technology and learns about the roles and responsibilities of technical support staff.
- At the start of class, initiate a frank discussion to set rules, guidelines, and standards. Once procedures have been established, consistently uphold them.
- Make sure each site is properly equipped with functional and accessible equipment. Provide a toll-free hot line for reporting and rectifying problems.
- If course materials are sent by mail, make sure they are received well before class begins. To help students keep materials organized, consider binding the syllabus, handouts, and other readings prior to distribution.
- Start off slowly with a manageable number of sites and students. The logistical difficulties of distant teaching increase with each additional site.

Figure 9.1. Teaching on Instructional Television
SOURCE: University of Idaho College of Engineering (1995a).

It is important for faculty to be prepared if they will be teaching an instructional television course. University of Maryland University College recommends that faculty be trained on the use of technology. Faculty are likely to be more confident and effective if they understand what they are being asked to do, and why. University of Maryland University College recommends that orientation and training should be scheduled well in advance of the beginning of the semester to give faculty sufficient time to redesign, modify, or adapt their course and assignments specifically to the new delivery mode.

Two-Way Interactive Video Teleconferencing

Video teleconferencing is an improvement on one-way instructional television because it provides the opportunity for the students at the remote site to see and interact with the instructor. The technology used for video teleconferencing is different. Most teleconferencing systems use digital telephone lines as the means of connecting. These are special telephone lines, either T-1 or Integrated Services Digital Network (ISDN), that allow the high-speed transmission of digital data. Some universities also allow for multisite connecting, allowing the instructor

- Turn on the CODEC and the monitors.
- Dial the distant site(s) to establish a link.
- Control camera focus and field at the origination site and at the distant site(s).
- Adjust the volume to an acceptable level.
- Dial out to a remote location.
- Select the appropriate data rate.
- Reset "echo canceling" capability.
- Switch to and from the document camera.
- Switch to and from the computer output.
- Use a computer to generate and display multimedia presentations.
- Use the VCR to broadcast a video for all locations.
- Terminate the link with the distant site(s).
- Shut down the equipment.

Figure 9.2. Working With Videoconferencing Equipment
SOURCE: University of Idaho College of Engineering (1995b).

to interact with more than one site at a time. Video teleconferencing uses devices called compression-decompression (CODEC) that convert the video signal to digital data. There are some technical problems with video teleconferencing as a teaching medium. Video compression tends to cause blurring in the image, particularly if there is a lot of motion. In addition, there may be a slight delay in the audio that takes getting used to.

Because a teacher can see and hear remote learners in real time, he or she can use conversation and body language to enhance communication. Frequent interaction increases understanding and encourages more personalized instruction. Interactive teaching strategies such as questioning and discussion can also help engage and motivate learners by making them active participants. Remote experts can also be connected to the class and can help validate understanding, provide feedback, and introduce practical examples (Woodruff & Mosby, 1996).

The University of Idaho College of Engineering recommends that an instructor be taught how to use all features of the equipment. Some of the critical operations that an instructor should be capable of performing are listed in Figure 9.2.

E-Mail and Listserv

E-mail is now widely available to students and faculty at most colleges and universities. Even at smaller colleges that do not provide e-mail support, many faculty and students have e-mail through Internet

Service Providers (ISPs) such as America Online, Prodigy, or CompuServe. Some universities are beginning to get out of providing e-mail support and requiring students to get e-mail from an ISP as a requirement for enrollment. For example, University of Maryland University College has worked out an agreement with several ISPs to offer discounts to enrolled students.

Several mailing programs make it possible to set up a mailing list or mail reflector. These create electronic addresses that forward an e-mail message to everyone on the list. There are essentially two types of mail reflectors. One is a closed list in which names and addresses can be entered only by the list administrator. The other type of list is a subscription list. An individual sends a message to the list indicating that he or she would like to join. This second type of mail reflector is generically called a *listserv*. Listserv is a specific software package. Other packages that do the same job include Majordomo and Listproc. The University of Maryland School of Nursing uses a package called BeroList. It automatically creates a Web page that archives all the class e-mail, providing students and faculty with access to the electronic conversation.

Mail reflectors generally require a UNIX computer and campus computing support. Many colleges provide mail reflector support through their academic computing departments.

There are several advantages to setting up a class list. First of all, it allows the class conversation to continue outside the classroom. In a traditional campus class, students and instructor generally meet only 3 hours per week in a classroom. With an e-mail list for the class, the instructor can continue the class conversation throughout the week. One technique is to use the e-mail list as a 1-minute paper. At the end of class, the instructor asks students to submit to the class list a 1-minute paper stating what they thought the most important point was in class that day. In addition, students are asked what they would like to cover in class at the next meeting. This technique gives students a chance to compare what they thought was most important with what their classmates thought was most important.

Another e-mail technique for class is the question of the week. Every week, students must look for the instructor's question of the week on e-mail—usually a question related to the class's recent activities or to the assignment for the week. This enables class dialogue to continue throughout the week and keeps students focused.

E-mail is a great equalizer among students. Inevitably in class, a few extroverted students tend to dominate classroom conversation and ask a lot of questions. Also inevitably, students tend to be introverted and not to interact much in class. E-mail lists equalize these two extremes. The quiet students are heard equally as well as the extroverted students.

There are disadvantages to e-mail lists. Students and faculty may struggle with the technology. If the class mail reflector is a list-serve to which students must subscribe, sometimes they have trouble correctly accomplishing this. Students may also have problems logging into their e-mail accounts. With many mail reflectors, it's very easy to send out a message to the entire class to when you intend to send a private message to one individual. In addition, there is the phenomenon of "flaming": having a strong emotional response to an e-mail message and quickly sending a fiery message in response before the emotional reaction has passed. It is important to have classroom policies with regard to flaming.

Finally, there is the disadvantage of faculty workload with regard to classroom e-mail. Most instructors who use classroom e-mail lists agree that they improve the quality of education in the class. The downside is that a tremendous amount of time is required to read all the e-mail. Some faculty members report that it doubles their workload for the class. There are techniques for controlling the problem, however. For example, it will probably not be possible to answer every single student message posted to the class list. Therefore, it may be appropriate to establish a class policy for the instructor to read all the mail but to respond only to selected messages. Encourage students to respond to each other if they know the answer.

The Web and Classroom Resources

The Internet began in the late 1960s as the Advanced Research Projects Agency of the United States Department of Defense. This was known as ARPAnet; it was created to provide a data-switching network to connect mainframe computers at research institutions across the United States. Data at that time were mostly plain text. In late 1990, Tim Berners-Lee invented the WWW while working at CERN, the European Particle Physics Laboratory in Geneva, Switzerland. He developed the first WWW browser and the first WWW server, along with most of the communications software defining universal resource locators (URLs),

Hyper Text Transfer Protocol (HTTP), and Hyper Text Markup Language (HTML). Today, it is impossible to see a movie or a television commercial without also being given a Web address to contact for further information. Because of the wealth of information available on the Web and because of the ease of access, the Web is becoming an indispensable part of higher education, both in the classroom and in the virtual university.

It is a relatively easy matter to create class resources on the Web. It requires an account on a Web server, which customarily is maintained by the academic computing department of the campus. Several products are available that automatically translate a word processing document to HTML, the language of the Web. For example, Microsoft's Office 97 Word has the translation feature built in. Netscape 4.0 comes equipped with Netscape Composer, which not only supports the creation of the Web document in a word processor format but also supports transferring the page up to the Web account.

Perhaps the biggest problem with the Web is the excess of information. According to Stauffer (1996), one common problem in hypertext systems, especially with novices, is disorientation, or becoming lost in the links. A number of advanced navigational tools prevent this. Punctual aids, such as transport buttons, and help buttons assist the learner to move forward. Stauffer also notes that structural aids, such as maps, filters, and indexes, help the student view the overall structure. Historical aids show users where they have been.

Confusion and disorientation are compounded by the rush of colleges and universities to place their course materials on-line. To help sort out this confusion and to create standards of quality for on-line courses, several universities and private corporations have begun producing Web-based course shells, called "courseware." These shells provide an organizing structure for the course, with appropriate navigational buttons for the students. One section of the shell may be for the syllabus, another section may be for course notes, and yet another section may be for the archive of the class's e-mail. Norman (1997) cites several courseware shells, including

- WebCT: University of British Columbia:
  http://homebrew1.cs.ubc.ca/webct
- RealEducation:
  http://realeducation.com

- Chalk by The Interactive Factory:
  http://www.chalk.com
- Web Course in a Box:
  http://madduck.mmd.vcu.edu/wcb
- TopClass from WBT Systems:
  http://www.wbtsystems.com

The very nature of a hyperlinked medium such as the Web lends itself to experiential, exploratory, and student-driven education based on the educational theory of constructivism. Instructors play more the role of facilitator and less the role of lecturer. At least one courseware shell, eWeb, attempts to support a constructivist approach to learning. eWeb is an integrated Web-based education environment that facilitates both intraschool and interschool collaboration as well as individualized learning (Zhao, n.d.). Although eWeb has tools explicitly designed to help students develop higher-order thinking skills through collaboration, it also allows teachers to develop and administer objective tests.

CU-SeeMe

CU-SeeMe is a free video conferencing program (under copyright of Cornell University) available to anyone with a Macintosh or Windows system and a connection to the Internet. Using a small, inexpensive camera attached to a computer, it is possible to see and talk with several people simultaneously anywhere in the world. Fetterman (1996) notes that Internet videoconferencing has certain benefits. For example, electronic communication is a little more personal and a lot more effective when you can hear the nuances of tone and see nonverbal language such as gestures and expressions, cues you normally depend on in face-to-face interactions.

CU-SeeMe does not provide an excellent video image, and there is a noticeable delay in the audio. One college instructor has described it as "like talking to an astronaut on the Apollo moon shot." It is not an ideal medium for lectures, but its potential is in how it enhances connectivity between student and instructor and between students. This is particularly true if it's used in conjunction with a distance learning program. In that case, it can be used as a connectivity tool to enable students to collaborate together at a distance.

❖ INTELLECTUAL PROPERTY

Many college instructors feel uncomfortable about publishing their course resources on the Web. They view their course materials as their intellectual property, and if they were to publish their course materials electronically, they would lose control of their materials. According to Field (1996), copyright arises automatically as soon as some aspect of a protectable work has been fixed in a tangible medium (such as an Internet server). Notice is not required; registration is required only if legal action is warranted and the work originates in the United States. Despite these protections, however, faculty may still be concerned that their own work is being made too public without adequate compensation being paid to them.

Consider this scenario:

Scenario

Professor Thomas has been asked to develop an on-line course on urban architecture to be delivered over the Web. Using a courseware shell, she develops the syllabus, assignments, and other materials, which she publishes on-line. She is fortunate because her school has a media center that is able to help her develop graphics. In addition, she has taken videotape footage of several examples germane to her topic. Working with the media center and another colleague who has skills in computer-aided instruction, she puts her video materials on an interactive CD-ROM that the school sells to students for $100 per copy as required materials for the course. Professor Thomas is delighted to learn she has 50 students enrolled. "That means there'll be $5,000 in sales from the CD," she thinks. "I wonder who will get that money?"

In this scenario, it is clear that the course contains the intellectual property of Professor Thomas. But she did not develop the material alone. In the traditional paradigm of instruction, the faculty member was very much a lone wolf who would be expected to develop course material and then stand up and teach it—also alone—to students. But in developing electronic multimedia instruction, the faculty member often is merely a member of a design team that works together to develop instructional materials for publication.

It is important that faculty members meet with administrators to establish protocols for electronic publishing and establishing who owns the materials once they are developed. Furthermore, it will be important to establish what rights the faculty member will have to materials once they are developed and who controls the materials once the faculty member leaves the school.

❖ FACULTY WORKLOAD

The time required to develop Web-based materials and ancillary CD-ROMs for electronic courses is substantial. In addition, the effort required to deliver an electronic course is enormous because much of the interaction is text based via e-mail. Traditional models of faculty workload and compensation will not translate very well into the era of the virtual university. Faculty may become more like independent contractors to the university, like doctors who are contracted to a health maintenance organization (Brown & Duguid, 1996). Faculty might be paid on a per capita basis, being rewarded for the number of students they attract.

Because electronic publishing and the development of multimedia are new, traditional policies for the promotion and tenure of faculty do not recognize such endeavors toward academic promotion. Colleges and universities need to examine their policies with regard to these issues.

❖ CONCLUSION

Technology is expanding students' ability to have greater access to resources at school, at home, and at work. Tools such as instructional television, e-mail, and the Web allow students the freedom to engage in learning independent of time and space, at the same time improving the quality of how they interact with the material, with the instructor, and with each other. These tools allow the whole world to become students' exploratorium. At the same time, the demands on new faculty members have never been greater. Faculty are expected to develop new on-line courses and to deliver them. Technology holds the promise for improving how faculty and their students learn, but colleges and universities need to establish modern and appropriate policies on intellectual property rights, faculty workload, and faculty compensation.

❖ REFERENCES

Bandura, A. (1977). *Social learning theory.* Englewood Cliffs, NJ: Prentice Hall.

Brown, J. S., & Duguid, P. (1996, July/August). Universities in the digital age. *Change, 28*(4), 11-19. (ERIC Document Reproduction Service No. EJ529592)

Dettrick, G. W. (n.d.). *Constructivist teaching strategies.*
http://www.inform.umd.edu/UMS+State/UMD-Projects/MCTP/Essays/Strategies.txt

Egan, M. W., Welch, M., Page, B., & Sebastian, J. (1992). Learners' perceptions of instructional delivery systems: Conventional and television. *American Journal of Distance Education, (6)*2, 47-55.

Fetterman, D. (1996). *Videoconferencing on-line: Enhancing communication over the Internet.*
http://cu-seeme.cornell.edu/Fetterman.html

Field, T. G. (1996). *Avoiding patent, copyright & trademark problems: What you don't know can hurt you!*
http://www.fplc.edu/tfield/aVoid.htm#Int

Hanley, S. (1994). *On constructivism.*
http://www.inform.umd.edu/UMS+State/UMD-Projects/MCTP/Essays/Constructivism.txt

Norman, K. (1997). *Teaching in the switched on classroom.*
http://www.lap.umd.edu/SOC/sochome.html

Romiszowski, A. J. (1986). *Developing auto-instructional materials.* London: Kogen Page.

Shneiderman, B. (1993). *Education by engagement and construction: Experiences in the AT&T teaching theater.*
http://www.inform.umd.edu/UMS+State/UMD-Projects/MCTP/Essays/EngagementAndConstruction.txt

Skinner, B. F. (1986). Programmed instruction revisited. *Phi Delta Kappan, 68*(2), 103-110.

Stauffer, K. (1996). *Student modeling and Web-based learning systems.*
http://ccism.pc.athabascau.ca/html/students/stupage/Project/initsm.htm

University of Idaho College of Engineering. (1995a). *Distance education at a glance guide 2.*
http://www.uidaho.edu/evo/dist2.html

University of Idaho College of Engineering. (1995b). Distance education at a glance guide 11.
http://www.uidaho.edu/evo/dist11.html#instructional

University of Maryland University College. (1996). *Models of distance education: A conceptual planning tool developed by the University of Maryland System Institute for Distance Education.*
   http://www.umuc.edu/ide/modlmenu.html#faculty

Woodruff, M., & Mosby, J. (1996). *A brief description of videoconferencing: Videoconferencing in the classroom and library.*
   http://www.kn.pacbell.com/wired/vidconf/description.html#what

Zhao, Y. (n.d.). *Web-based education environment: Conceptualization.*
   http://zhao.educ.msu.edu/eweb/theories/ewebarticle.html

10

Diversity in Higher Education

Mary Hatwood Futrell
Walter A. Brown

This chapter is for individuals in higher education, especially faculty members, who will play a major role in shaping the future of this country. It is an attempt to develop a deeper understanding among college and university (hereafter referred to as university) faculty and staff of how the current trends and events related to diversity reflect the reality of and their influences on the future of the United States. It looks carefully at the fact that, as Harold Hodgkinson (1996) says in *Bringing Tomorrow Into Focus*, the ankle bone is truly connected to the toe bone. Addressing the issue of diversity is also an opportunity to understand that the UNI-versity is the one place where a MULTI-versity of opinions and points of view can be heard and addressed.

❖ THE MANY FACES OF DIVERSITY

By its very definition, diversity implies that we are a varied people with varied opinions and ideas, that there are differences among and between us. Those differences are complex and may be viewed from many perspectives. Issues of culture, race, ethnicity, age, gender and sexual orientation, religion, socioeconomic status, class, political persuasions, disabilities, language, and geography define us individually and as a nation. E. T. Hall (1981) says that "we must stop ranking both people and talents and accept the fact that there are many roads to truth and no culture (group) has a corner on the path or is better equipped than others to search for it" (p. 7). Our diversity is who we are and defines who we hope to become.

The primary purpose of this chapter is to encourage faculty to explore ways that will allow higher education institutions, and ultimately America, to achieve unity out of our increased diversity. If each university commits to achieving this goal without destroying the beauty and strengths of the variances that define us, then we will have cause to celebrate the major factor that makes this nation unique.

❖ RESPONDING TO THE NEEDS OF A DIVERSE STUDENT BODY

Today, because of our increased diversity, the United States is frequently characterized as a nation of the world. For example, during the last decade, 9 million people immigrated to this country. This was the highest rate of immigration since the turn of the century. Most of the immigrants came from South and Central America and Asia. Only 15% came from Europe. In Figure 10.1, growth in diversity is projected to continue well into the 21st century.

Contrary to popular belief, today's immigrants do not simply settle in our large cities or coastal areas. Rather, immigrant populations are found in urban, suburban, and rural communities throughout the country. Nowhere is their presence felt stronger than in our education system. Preschools through graduate schools are feeling the enormous effect of these demographic changes. In Fairfax County, Virginia, a very affluent suburban school district with more than 150,000 students, more than 120 different languages are spoken. The public schools have responded by creating programs such as English as a second language to help immigrant students assimilate more quickly into the mainstream.

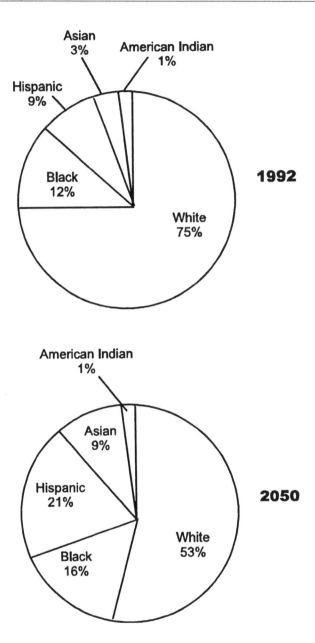

Figure 10.1. Diversity Pie Charts
SOURCE: Bureau of the Census.

Colleges and universities are also modifying their facilities, programs, and services to provide better support for students. These services may range from providing access ramps and elevators for students with physical disabilities to providing translation services for the hearing impaired to providing additional advisers for international students to granting students permission to form social or political organizations. As an example, across the river from Fairfax County at The George Washington University, special arrangements have been made to provide space for students from different religious faiths so they may worship throughout the week.

One of the demographic trends universities (and society as a whole) are beginning to recognize is aging. As Americans live longer and more enjoy good health, an increasing number are enrolling in postsecondary programs, especially at the university level. The swelling enrollment of elderly people on university campuses underscores the need for universities to design programs and other educational services for them. A visit to a typical campus classroom reflects this demographic shift. Seated in class along with the traditional 18- to 22-year-olds may be students in their 60s or 70s. These senior citizens epitomize what we mean by life-long learning. As Ken Dychtwald says, "the education system is going to have to be revamped for continual learning and reignition of people's brain cells" (cited in Cohen, 1997, p. 10).

The message seems clear. Trends and events indicate that America is becoming more, not less, diverse. This paradigm shift has major implications for our economic, political, social, and cultural institutions.

Our ability to recognize the reality and potential of diversity, often defined as multiculturalism, means that we need to move toward becoming a more intercultural society. How this intercultural society will be defined depends to a large degree on the roles and responses of colleges and universities in helping the nation address this issue.

We at universities need to find indicators and incentives for developing interactions and interchanges between and among groups that are dynamic and cooperative and that will lead to a more intercultural society. Achieving campus diversity, not fragmentation, will depend on our willingness and ability to design and implement policies and programs aimed at helping us constructively achieve this goal.

❖ ACHIEVING DIVERSITY

Where should we as university administrators, faculty, and students start? Perhaps the first place is by recognizing that each of us is a diverse, complex person. Just how do we achieve this recognition at the university level? One way is through the curriculum.

One particular graduate-level educational foundations course is taught by an interdisciplinary team that includes five faculty members. The team objective is to help students understand and appreciate diversity from a historic and futuristic perspective. The students enrolled in this yearlong course form a cohort that represents the major program areas (i.e., teacher preparation and special education, counseling, administration, policy studies, human resource development, international education, and museum education) in the Graduate School of Education and Human Development at The George Washington University. For many, it is the first time they have been in a course where most of the students are not from their specialty area. The course is based on six central themes: diversity, ethics and values, foundations of education, leadership, human development, and research.

We often start the diversity unit by asking the students how they define themselves and how they define diversity. Usually the response includes descriptors such as age, ethnicity, family, and professional interests. In other words, students respond by reciting their "age, rank, and serial number," so to speak. We then spend time discussing their personal definitions of diversity. The initial response is to discuss race, gender, and, perhaps, religion.

Eventually, we begin to talk about diversity from a broader, more historical perspective as well as diversity within and among diversity. To help students understand the micro- and macroissues involved in the interrelatedness of diversity issues, visuals are used to illustrate that we are far more diverse and complex than individuals and societies might at first blush realize. The visuals presented in Figures 10.2 and 10.3 and Table 10.1 are also used to portray the micro- and macroworlds in which we live. In other words, the program is designed to enable students to explore ethnic identity, cultural values, and beliefs in the context of self, family, social groups, and community.

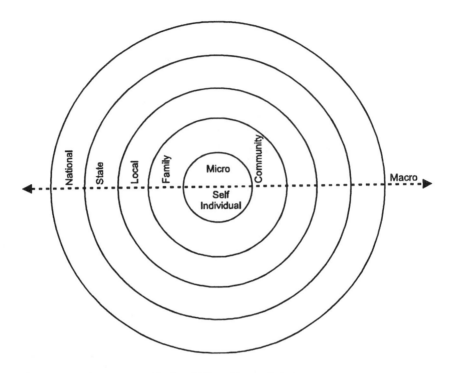

Figure 10.2. Concentric Circle of Micro-Macro Relations

One purpose of the diversity theme is to help students learn that understanding and appreciating one's own multiple cultures are related to characteristics that one shares with others, such as gender, race, ethnicity, national identity, religion, class, age, and even geography. Using one of the professors as an example, we discuss the fact that she is an African American woman who often feels the tension between being an African American and being a female. We also discuss the fact that within this racial and ethnic grouping are wide ranges of hues of color, religious, socioeconomic, and political persuasions. For example, she listens to classical, jazz, and country western music as well as rhythm and blues. Her tastes for foods are equally diverse. We discuss perceptions and differences among groups and the difficulties of overcoming our inhibitions about others who may be different (or we think they are) from our own group.

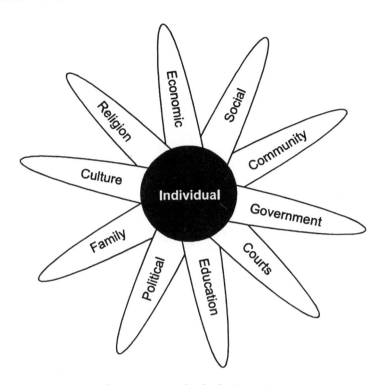

Figure 10.3. Factors Influencing an Individual's Diversity

Because the cohort represents all program areas in the school, the students are asked to identify what they perceive to be major issues related to diversity that need to be addressed within their specialty areas and in society. Some of the issues identified are inclusion; affirmative action; intolerance; poverty; the "us" versus "them" mentality; resistance from exclusion of white males; lack of understanding about implications of the influx of refugees and immigrants; gay and lesbian rights; hate crimes; increased classism; the overemphasis on racism, sexism, and other isms; and the potential for fragmentation rather than unity. Students also raise concerns about their ability to develop a rapport with students or clients who are from ethnic or racial groups other than their own.

The issues identified are then used for subsequent class discussions to help students understand how diversity affects them personally and

TABLE 10.1 Characteristics of Diversity/Pluralism/Multiculturalism Diversity Within Diversity

Factors Influencing Diversity	Race	Ethnicity	Class	Language	Sex/Gender	Exceptionalities	Age	Religion	Geography	Physical Shape	Ideology
Race											
Ethnicity											
Class											
Language											
Sex/Gender											
Exceptionalities											
Age											
Religion											
Geography											
Physical Shape											
Ideology											

professionally. For example, students are urged to expand their knowledge about and become more sensitive to diversity-related issues personally, especially regarding the students or clients with whom they will be entrusted to work. This is done through self-study (i.e., reading), visiting places of religious worship or museums, traveling, and working with different groups.

Do we solve all the issues? Of course not, but as a result of the discussions, these students will be more willing to confront these and other diversity-related issues. Enhanced appreciation is also achieved by the integration of diversity issues with the other themes that form the foundation of the course.

This course is successful because of the commitment of the faculty and administration to ensure that graduates have understanding, appreciation, and respect for cultural diversity in communities (whether local, state, or national) where they will be living and working. It is the hope that graduates and the clients to whom they will be responsible understand that we do indeed live in an intercultural, interdependent society.

❖ DIVERSITY AMONG FACULTY AND STUDENTS

Designing and implementing culturally responsive pedagogy and curricular offerings is one way of responding to the diversity theme. Achieving campus diversity is dependent on the willingness of faculty to design and implement programs that support this goal. It is also dependent on successful efforts to recruit and retain faculty and students who reflect the diversity we celebrate.

Recruiting a Diverse Student Body

First, let's address the issue of recruiting and enrolling students from diverse groups. Demographic trends indicate that today, approximately 30% of all K-12 students are from groups that historically have been identified as underrepresented in our society (African American, Hispanic American, Native American, and Asian American). This is expected to increase to 35% to 40% within the next two decades. According to a report titled "Conditions of Minorities in Higher Education" (see Department of Education, 1997), of these students, 54% indicated they planned to attend college. The *Almanac* (Chronicle of Higher Education,

1996) reports, however, that of the 14 million students enrolled in our colleges and universities, only 24% represent minority groups.

There are a variety of reasons why so few students of color actually matriculate to college and why even fewer remain there once enrolled. One reason may be that many of these students do not have the resources to attend college because of lower family incomes. This problem could be further exacerbated as a result of the recent renewed attacks on affirmative action programs.

Affirmative action has become a hot topic of discussion on campuses as colleges and universities struggle to diversify their student bodies, faculty, and administration. According to an article in the *Chronicle of Higher Education* (Lederman, 1997), recent court and referendum decisions in California, Maryland, Mississippi, Virginia, and Texas have nullified university affirmative action programs that were race and gender specific. In addition, in August 1996, Congress almost passed a bill that would have eliminated college financial aid to all immigrant noncitizens, legal or undocumented.

It is anticipated that students in these targeted populations, particularly those from minority and low-income groups, will be affected negatively by these decisions. The future is already here, however. The effect is already being felt in graduate programs, especially in law and medical schools, across the nation as enrollments for students from minority groups have decreased dramatically. The loss of affirmative action programs is expected to also negatively affect undergraduate enrollments.

This change is occurring at a time when the demand for more and better education for all citizens is necessary for America to remain competitive in the 21st century. Consequently, it is critical to ensure that members of underrepresented groups are included in the mainstream of our society through opportunities in higher education. As the Council of Graduate Schools (1997) so eloquently states, a primary goal of higher education is "to engage in intellectual activities that engender respect for intellect regardless of source, and build a community whose members are judged by the quality of their ideas." The world in which today's graduates will work is a changing world where race, gender, ethnicity, nationality, and related factors merge with knowledge, merit, and talent to play important roles in shaping society. Even if colleges and universities are not able to maintain their affirmative action programs, they do have a moral responsibility to sustain goals that will promote a diverse student and faculty population on campus.

Students must first be prepared adequately for college- and university-level work. A major impediment to diversity in education is the growing number of students from minority and low-income families, as well as immigrant students who are in public schools (K-12) that are resource poor and racially and socioeconomically segregated. This is particularly alarming in our inner cities, where 98% of African American and Hispanic American students attend segregated schools. All too often, these schools do not have the resources to provide the high-quality staff, curricular programs, technologies, and other resources found in more affluent school districts. Thus, once again the opportunities are lacking that would ensure that students from resource-poor and increasingly racially segregated school districts have the knowledge and skills necessary to succeed in college.

Diversity is also hindered by the quality of education (inner-city) minority and low-income students receive at the K-12 level. Although a recent government report shows that "students from all minority groups are enrolled in a more rigorous curriculum than in the past" (cited in Viadero, 1995), Oakes, Orfield, and Slavins have shown that too many of these students are tracked into low-ability classes. Thus, although these students may desire to go to college, many have not received the educational foundation that will allow them to achieve a high score on gatekeeper indicators such as the SAT or ACT or to negotiate the higher education system once admitted. For instance, if students do not have a firm grasp of mathematics or strong reading comprehension on leaving high school, they will be at a disadvantage when trying to master technical material in college. If these issues are addressed with serious intent at the local school district level, at the elementary and secondary school levels, then universities will not have to allocate above-average funding to remedial programs just to bring students up to academic standards.

A number of colleges and universities have begun to form partnerships with schools and school districts to work with teachers, administrators, parents, and students to reduce and overcome these obstacles. One example is the partnership between Virginia Polytechnic Institute and State University (VPI&SU) and the Roanoke (VA) City Public Schools. VPI&SU joined forces with the public schools, parents, religious, and other community groups to work with academically gifted students from minority and low-income families. Students receive counseling from university faculty regarding their career aspirations and the curricular program to study in high school to achieve their goal, participate in tutoring, and make visits to the VPI&SU campus to attend cultural, athletic, and other activities. In addition, special summer seminars are held to help students learn how to adjust to campus life and to address areas where they may be academically deficient. Students who complete the program and attain the grade point average and test scores required for admission are eligible for scholarships to support them if they attend VPI&SU.

Approximately 130 colleges and universities have similar outreach programs to inform public school staff and students about university expectations and opportunities. These programs are designed to help ensure that university student populations do indeed reflect the diversity that defines America. Such programs also indicate that, as a nation, we will be able to draw on the enhanced talents and abilities of all Americans.

Diversity Among University Faculty

Vital to the success of the college or university and its students is the need to ensure that faculty and staff reflect the diversity that defines our nation. Yet, data from the *Digest of Educational Statistics* (Department of Education, 1995) indicate that of the 500,000 university faculty around the country, only 32% are women and 13% are minorities. When we examine the issues of promotion and rank, we discover that women represent only 16% of all faculty ranked at the full professor level. For faculty from minority groups, the numbers are more ominous, with only 10% achieving the rank of full professor.

As we discuss the need to enhance diversity within and among the student population, it is equally important to work toward concurrent change at the faculty level. Although it is imperative for all faculty to possess the ability to advise, teach, and work effectively with a diverse student population, there is also a critical need to ensure that students have opportunities to work with faculty who reflect intellectual diversity. Faculty members from a wide spectrum of experiences and training (e.g., racial, ethnic, religious, gender, political) enrich the intellectual experiences of students. As Edgar Beckham (1997) points out,

Diversity has not been merely a matter of demographics. It has also been an intellectual venture. Just as demographic diversity has increased hand in hand with the expansion of educational opportunity for all, the increasing diversity of knowledge has been part of the knowledge explosion and has enriched the curriculum and made it more challenging. (p. 58)

Thus, Cornel West, Gary Orfield, Linda Darling-Hammond, Robert Slavins, Sarah Lawrence Lightfoot, Ronald Takaki, Thomas Sowell, Laura Rendon, Alfredo Dela, Mildred Garcia, and Arthur Schleshinger, to name a few, bring not only their expertise as recognized academicians but also experiences and perspectives from their cultural backgrounds. Surely, for example, Toni Morrison's work has been influenced by the works of Shakespeare just as our understanding of Shakespeare's plays and sonnets have been influenced by Morrison's works. Each faculty member in his or her own way expands and enriches the educational experiences of the students he or she teaches and the faculty with whom he or she works.

Techniques to Fulfill the Goal of a Diverse Faculty

For many minorities and women, becoming a member of the professorate at majority institutions is equivalent to feeling like a window dresser or getting caught in a revolving door and every few years moving on to another university. Promotion and tenure is often a lonely and barren process, particularly for minority and female faculty members. Yet this does not have to be.

Many minority and female faculty members are shut out of the "club" of more senior faculty members or are excluded from informal work groups where the real political and academic decisions are made. As a result, minority and female faculty members may not have opportunities to network with key faculty. This exclusion could lead to an inability to build strong support among faculty, which is critical to achieving promotion or tenure.

At the same time, minority and female faculty members may have to address issues of bias in their efforts to secure a position, be promoted, or receive tenure. Some research suggests that bias is most effectively decreased not only through education but also by exposure to and experience with members of the opposite sex and other groups. Bias is also decreased by applying the golden rule: Treat others as you would have them treat you. In other words, treat people with respect and dignity and in an unbiased way.

Changing the climate of the culture within our higher education institutions is indeed an educational experience. It is also one to which each of us must be committed. In addition to the equal employment opportunity statement required by federal law, every school and university should have a clearly articulated policy that is a proactive commitment to faculty diversity. This policy should be reflected in the mission statement, goals, and other official documents of the institution. A written policy is not enough, however. It must be a living policy with clearly articulated strategies for its achievement and whose implementation will enhance, not decrease, faculty diversity.

Recruitment efforts should include targeting audiences that will yield viable candidates for faculty positions. Incentives, opportunities for professional development, and career development are techniques to help address issues related to the recruitment, retention, and promotion of all faculty, especially minorities and females. In addition, career management opportunities and support groups are effective techniques to use in an effort to create diversity among faculty. The point is, strengthening faculty diversity within our schools requires a commitment that goes beyond simply having a written policy. It takes leadership from academic administrators committed to the process.

When a faculty member is hired, one of the first documents he or she should receive is a copy of the criteria for promotion and tenure. The department chair and/or school administration should carefully explain the procedures and be accessible to clarify them further if necessary. Second, the new faculty member should ask for or be assigned a senior faculty member who will mentor him or her through at least the first few years as a member of the faculty. Efforts should be made to provide support and resources to enable the junior faculty member to define and complete his or her research agenda, design new curricular offerings, and become involved in students' thesis and dissertation work.

Further, junior faculty members should not be overwhelmed with administrative duties. It is very important for junior faculty members to understand they do have a right to say no if their ability to teach and conduct research is thwarted because other demands placed on them are becoming unreasonable. Because they are new, junior faculty members often feel obligated to accept responsibilities that their senior counterparts refuse to fulfill.

Junior faculty members should be supported in their efforts to earn promotion and/or tenure. This can be done through a variety of ways without compromising the integrity of the process. For instance, during the first year, junior faculty members could be given a reduced course load to ensure that they have sufficient time to become an integral part of the faculty, establish their research agenda, publish scholarly works, develop curricula, adjust to advising students, improve their teaching, and so forth. After all, universities are supposed to be learning communities that nurture the professional growth and development of their faculty and students.

Successfully cultivating a more diverse faculty also means making sure they know what services and programs are available to help them be more successful in teaching and advising students, fulfilling their research agenda, publishing, and becoming an integral member of the university and professional community.

❖ SUMMARY

As David Imig (1995), executive director of the American Association of Colleges of Teacher Education, stated,

> Playing a prominent role in the campus debates about affirmative action, examining admissions and retention policies for students, assessing faculty recruitment and promotion and tenure policies relative to their effect on the commitment to diversity, must be high on the agenda for all colleges and universities.

The technological and economic transformation occurring in America is also transforming our colleges and universities. At the same time, changing demographics will have no less a transforming effect on America's institutions of higher education—demographics that reflect the fact that our population is becoming older on the one hand while becoming younger and more diverse on the other. Neither phenomenon can be ignored. The central mission of our colleges and universities is directly linked with the future of diversity in America.

These two changes, which appear to be in conflict with one another, demand that more than ever before we learn to live and work together. According to Hodgkinson (1996), there are currently 3.4 workers per retiree, soon to be 2.0. By 2011, 70 million more Americans will retire or will be eligible to do so.

The issue of diversity is an educational as well as an economic issue we ignore at our peril. How colleges and universities respond will indeed shape the economic, legal, political, and social structures that define our society, the very fabric of our future as a democracy. President Bill Clinton reflected this sentiment in his June 14, 1997, speech on race relations in America, stating, "I believe a student body that reflects the excellence and the diversity of the people we will live and work together with has independent and educational value" (p. A8). As John Dewey (1990) emphasizes, school and society are one, and higher education is intertwined with what he terms the *dilemmas* and the *perplexities of its time*. Institutions of higher learning must join in the effort to build communities for the new millennium that reflect the sociocultural realities that define us, not just for moral reasons but also for enlightened self-interest.

❖ REFERENCES

Beckham, E. R. (1997, January 5). Diversity opens doors to all. *New York Times, Education Life Supplement,* p. 58.

Building an inclusive graduate community: A statement of principles. (1997). *Communicator, 30*(5), 1-4.

Chronicle of Higher Education. (1996). *Almanac.* Washington, DC: Author.

Clinton, B. (1997, June 14). In building one America, all citizens must serve. Speech reprinted in *Washington Post,* p. A8.

Cohen, S. (1997, June 1). Old glory. *Washington Post Magazine,* pp. 6-11, 25-31.

Department of Education. (1995). *Digest of educational statistics 1995.* Washington, DC: Office of Educational Research and Improvement.

Department of Education. (1997). *Minorities in higher education: Findings from the condition of education 1996.* Washington, DC: Office of Educational Research and Improvement.

Dewey, J. (1990). *The school and society.* Chicago: University of Chicago Press.

Hall, E. T. (1981). *Beyond culture.* New York: Doubleday.

Hodgkinson, H. L. (1996, January). *Bringing tomorrow into focus: Demographic insights into the future.* Washington, DC: Institute for Educational Leadership, Center for Demographic Policy.

Imig, D. G. (1995, October). *American teacher education at a crossroads: Five educational trends demanding a response from schools of education.* Paper presented at the American Association of Colleges for Teacher Education Seminar, Washington, DC.

Lederman, D. (1997, January). With lawsuits pending, U. of California will again consider race in admissions. *Chronicle of Higher Education*, p. A30.

Viadero, D. (1995, September 20). Students chart big boost in course-taking. *Education Week*, pp. 1, 16.

❖ SUPPLEMENTAL READING

Applebome, P. (1997, March 26). Texas is told to keep affirmative action in universities or risk losing federal aid. *New York Times*, p. 11.

Arches, J., Darlington-Hope, M., Gerson, J., Gibson, J., Habana-Hafner, S., & Kiang, P. (1997). New voices in university-community transformation. *Change, 29*(1), 36-41.

Banks, J. A. (1996). Transformative knowledge, curriculum reform, and action. In J. A. Banks (Ed.), *Multicultural education, transformative knowledge and action: Historical and contemporary perspectives.* New York: Teachers College Press.

Bensimon, E. M., & Soto, M. (1997). Can we rebuild civic life without a multiracial university? *Change, 29*(1), 42-44.

European Union. (1997, May). *Opinion on intercultural education.* Paper presented as background documentation for Seminar on Intercultural Education in Geneva, Switzerland.

Gose, B. (1997, February 21). Gay students have their own floor in a U. of Massachusetts dormitory. *Chronicle of Higher Education*, pp. A37-38.

Howard, G. (1996). Whites in multicultural education: Rethinking our role. In J. A. Banks (Ed.), *Multicultural education, transformative knowledge and action: Historical and contemporary perspectives.* New York: Teachers College Press.

Hurtado, S. (1996). How diversity affects teaching and learning. *Educational Record, 7*(4), 27-29.

Mangan, K. S. (1997, January 10). Minority enrollments drop at medical schools. *Chronicle of Higher Education*, p. A49.

Morrison, A. M., & Von Glinow, M. A. (1990, February). Women and minorities in management. *American Psychologist, 45*(2), 200-208.

National Task Force for Minority Achievement in Higher Education. (1990). *Achieving campus diversity: Policies for change.* Denver, CO: Education Commission of the States.

Oakes, J. (1985). *Keeping track: How schools structure inequality.* New Haven, CT: Yale University Press.

Sanchez, R., & Pressley, S. A. (1997, May 19). Minority admissions fall with preferences ban. *Washington Post*, pp. A-1, A-11.

Slavins, R. E. (1990). *Cooperative learning: Theory, research, and practice.* Englewood Cliffs, NJ: Prentice Hall.

Thomas, D. A., & Ely, R. J. (1996). Making differences matter: A new paradigm for managing diversity. *Harvard Business Review, 74*(5), 79-90.

Epilogue

Neal Chalofsky
Virginia Bianco-Mathis

Dr. Johnson finished the second session of an experimental seminar that she recently designed. The dialogue among the students and herself was "awesome," with several of the students staying way past the end of the class to share some personal insights. She came home exhausted but excited. This is what it's all about, she thought. Getting settled in her favorite chair, she planned her next day, when she would be chairing a task force for her school on equality for contract faculty and then meeting with several faculty from other disciplines within the university to discuss a joint master's program. As she drifted off, her thoughts turned to her trip to Dublin on Sunday to present a paper at an international conference. Afterward, her husband would be joining her for a couple of days touring the countryside . . .

Is it always like this? Of course not. But it can be like this for a significant amount of the time if you are willing and able to shape the work to fit your professional needs and desires. You have to take charge of your academic life (which does not mean just taking care of yourself without regard for your colleagues). This means developing activities and relationships that are truly meaningful and fulfilling.

Although there are certainly cases of faculty who have been hurt by the "system," most of the faculty we know are relatively happy in academia. Compare that with studies that consistently report that approximately 85% of American workers are unhappy in their jobs.

Today's academic has much to juggle and many decisions to make. Fortunately, the profession offers a multitude of options, choices, and opportunities. The emergence of the virtual university is both unsettling and exciting. The variety of institutions, students, and programs is challenging. And discussions of tenure, contract appointments, and accountability are mounting.

The key—as the contributors of this book point out—is to manage your career. On a periodic basis, revisit your personal goals and adjust your environment accordingly. Thankfully, the academic landscape—unlike many others—is flexible. Shape it. Create it.

We believe, despite the expected frustrations and setbacks, that academic life is one of the few professions that allows individuals to follow and share inner passion: the love of continuous learning, discovery, and growth.

Index

About the Editors

Virginia Bianco-Mathis is Associate Professor in the School of Business, Graduate Programs, at Marymount University. She teaches courses in organization development, team and group dynamics, and human resource strategy. She coordinates the Human Resource Management and Organization Development master's programs and advises all interns. Previously, she held positions as Training Specialist for the Bell Telephone System, Manager of Training and Organization Development at Martin Marietta, and Vice President of Human Resources at the Artery Organization. Presently, she consults in areas of executive coaching, team building, organizational diagnosis, strategic planning, and performance management. Some of her clients include Mobil, the American Diabetes Association, LCC International, Century Computing, and the Department of State. She has an undergraduate degree from the University of Connecticut, a master's degree from Johns Hopkins University, and a doctorate from George Washington University. Her research involves the study of the dynamics of change and human development within organizations. She has given major presentations at several international conferences, including such titles as *A Multidisciplinary Approach to Implementing Total Quality and Change: Best Practices.*

In the past 2 years, she has published *Consulting Dilemmas, The Adjunct Faculty Handbook* (with Neal Chalofsky) and *Change in Organizations: Best Practices* (with Cynthia Roman).

Neal Chalofsky is Professor of the Human Resource Development (HRD) Graduate Program at George Washington University and director of the HRD Doctoral Program. His teaching responsibilities include foundations of HRD, group dynamics and facilitation, innovative learning techniques, consultation, and a special seminar on the meaning of work. His research interests include values and meaning of work, individual and group learning, and the development of the HRD profession. Previously, he was a Professor and Director of HRD graduate studies at Virginia Polytechnic Institute and State University (Virginia Tech). He has also been an internal HRD practitioner, manager, and researcher for several government and corporate organizations. He has consulted with such organizations as Mobil Research and Development Corporation, the Department of Education, Computer Sciences Corporation, the U.S. Chamber of Commerce, the Smithsonian Institution, Ernst & Young, Inc., the World Bank, the National Alliance of Business, and Bell Atlantic. His consultation interests are in the areas of establishing a culture in organizations based on meaningful work and learning, group facilitation and team development, program evaluation, and improving the organizational HRD function. He has been a member of the national board of directors and chair of several national committees of the American Society for Training and Development, as well as past president of the Washington, DC chapter. He is coauthor of *Effective Human Resource Development* and *Up the HRD Ladder,* as well as numerous chapters of edited works and journal articles. He is also a reviewer for *Human Resources Development Quarterly.*

About the Contributors

Rosemarie Bosler (Chapter 3, "Student Advising") is Associate Professor of Education at Trinity College in Washington, DC. She teaches courses in literacy education and cultural diversity. She is Co-Director of Trinity College's Urban Literacy Center, which prepares preservice and in-service teachers to work with at-risk youth in urban settings.

Walter A. Brown (Chapter 10, "Diversity in Higher Education") is Assistant Professor of Higher Education Administration at George Washington University. His areas of specialization are higher education finance and strategic planning. He has held posts with Fortune 100 corporations in the areas of finance and strategic planning; the Committee on the Budget, the U.S. House of Representatives; and as a finance faculty member and administrator at Bowie State University and the University of the District of Columbia, respectively. His research interests are strategic planning at large 4-year institutions, the financial stability of public and private institutions, and the progression of senior-level minority administrators and faculty at majority institutions.

Nyla Carney (Chapter 1, "Administration and Management") is Associate Dean for the School of Arts and Sciences and Professor of Language and Literature at Marymount University. She has more than 27 years of teaching and administrative experience in both state and private college and university systems. She has taught courses in Spanish, French, ESL, and linguistics. Her academic experience has included serving on various university governance committees, participating on search committees for faculty and administrative positions, Chair of Marymount's Intensive English program, and coordinator of Spanish and French departments at the community college level. She holds master's degrees from both the University of Illinois and the University of Wisconsin. Her doctorate is from Georgetown University.

Sharon Johnson Confessore (Chapter 8, "New Learning Approaches") is Associate Professor of Human Resource Development and Director of the Executive Leadership Program at George Washington University. She teaches courses in adult learning, management-executive learning, and professional development. She consults with various business and government agencies in the areas of learning and learning systems design. She received a PhD from the University of Oklahoma in Adult Learning and has more than 20 years experience in educational environments.

Sharon Ahern Fechter (Chapter 4, "Academic Research"), formerly Associate Dean for Liberal Studies, Continuing Studies, and Performing Arts, is Professor of Spanish and English as a Second Language at Mount Vernon College in Washington, DC. She also serves as the Director of Inter-Institutional Collaboration for Project 2001, a Mellon-funded project at Middlebury College that explores the use of technology in foreign language instruction in liberal arts institutions. She holds a PhD from New York University and has published texts for ESL and Spanish as well articles on various research topics in language, literature, and women's studies.

James J. Fletcher (Chapter 2, "Teaching and Learning") is a philosopher by training. He holds a PhD in philosophy from Indiana University. His doctoral work focused on establishing an objective basis for art criticism. His primary areas of interest in philosophy are ethics, philosophy of art, and philosophy of technology. He has been a member of the George Mason faculty since 1972, serving in a variety of teaching and administrative capacities. In 1982, he was asked to join the Office of Academic Affairs as Assistant Vice President and Dean for Undergraduate Studies; he later became Associate Provost. Among his responsibilities were academic policies, faculty development, undergraduate student appeals of honor code and academic matters, and liaison with the state council for higher education. In 1996, he left the Provost's Office to establish the University Project on Teaching and Learning, which he currently directs. His recent publications and presentations have been on issues related to higher education.

Mary Hatwood Futrell (Chapter 10, "Diversity in Higher Education"), an internationally known educator and former President of the National Education Association, became Dean of the Graduate School of Education and Human Development (GSEHD) in 1995. A George Washington University alumna, she is Associate Professor of educational policy studies and Director of the GSEHD Center for Curriculum, Standards, and Technology. In addition to her unprecedented 6-year term leading the NEA, she is a former President of the World Conference of Organizations of the Teaching Profession and currently President of Education International. She was a senior consultant for the Quality Education for Minorities Network and serves on the boards of the Carnegie Foundation for the Advancement of Teaching, Kettering Foundation, National Foundation for the Improvement of Education, and Institute for Educational Leadership.

Sharon L. Levin (Chapter 3, "Student Advising") is Assistant Professor of Business Administration at Trinity College in Washington, DC, where she teaches accounting, quantitative methods, and international business. In addition to classroom teaching, she also teaches international business courses abroad. As the Chair of the Division of Corporate and Community Affairs, she manages the business department of four graduate school departments. Before joining the academic community, she earned a CPA in 1988 and practiced accounting for 5 years. Her doctorate is from George Washington University, and her research is in the area of measuring organizational behavior.

Teresa Long (Chapter 1, "Administration and Management") is Professor of Economics and Chair of the Department of Accounting, Economics, and Finance at Marymount University, where she teaches macroeconomics and international economics. Her experience in higher education includes a 3-year term as Associate Dean of the School of Business, Chair of the Faculty Council and membership on promotion and tenure, budget and planning, admissions and academic standards, curriculum and instruction, and institutional self-study committees. She also serves on visiting teams for the regional accreditation organization. Her master's and doctorate degrees are from Iowa State University.

Rhonda J. Malone (Chapter 7, "Professional Development and Advancement") is currently Assistant to the Associate Provost for Faculty Affairs at the University of Maryland. In that capacity, she coordinates orientation and development programs for faculty and academic administrators. She also assists in the implementation of policies and procedures related to faculty matters, in particular matters related to promotion, tenure, and performance review. She holds an MEd from Kent State University and a PhD in higher education leadership and policy analysis from the University of Maryland. She consults with organizations and individuals on a variety of issues, including communication and feedback, organizational change, and career development.

William J. A. Marshall (Chapter 5, "University Service") is Professor and Chair of the Department of Administration and Supervision, Gallaudet University. Having served at the helm of the University Faculty Senate for almost 10 years, he currently trains doctoral students in special education administration. He was awarded the President's Distinguished University faculty member in 1990. He formerly taught at the University of Washington at Seattle and the University of Illinois at Champaign. He is the former Administrative Director at the Whitney Young Magnet High School in Chicago and the Dean/Director of the Model Secondary School for the Deaf on the campus of Gallaudet University. At press time, he was again re-elected for an unprecedented third three-year term as chair of the university faculty and university faculty Senate.

Karen L. Medsker (Chapter 6, "Professional Service") is Professor and Chair of the Human Resources Department in the School of Business Administration at Marymount University, where she teaches courses in instructional design, performance analysis and improvement, and evaluation. She earned a PhD in instructional systems from Florida State University, worked as an instructional technologist and training supervisor at AT&T Bell laboratories, and served as Director of Instructional Development at Indiana University-Purdue University at Indianapolis. She consults regularly with businesses and government agencies on training and performance improvement issues and is actively involved in professional service activities, primarily with the International Society for Performance Improvement and the American Society for Training and Development. She has written many articles and book chapters and coauthored *The Conditions of Learning: Training Applications* with Robert M. Gagné (1996).

Sondra K. Patrick (Chapter 2, "Teaching and Learning") coordinates Institutional Assessment at Marymount University (Arlington, VA) and teaches research methods courses at the Graduate School of Education and Human Development, George Washington University (Washington, DC). Her research focuses on issues related to technology, teaching and learning; institutional change in higher education; education in urban settings; and the visual representation of data. She consults for the Center for Excellence and Equity in Education and coordinated the qualitative evaluation of the 1998 D.C. Summer STARS program. She holds a PhD in education from George Mason University (Fairfax, VA).

Theodore E. Stone (Chapter 9, "Technology") is Director of the Office of Learning Technologies and Media Center for the University of Maryland School of Nursing in Baltimore. His main work is to seek out and implement new technologies that can improve the quality of how students learn. A large part of this work involves the development of Web-based and CD-ROM-based instruction and distance learning technology. He is also Assistant Professor in the Department of Education, Administration, Health Policy, and Informatics at the University of Maryland School of Nursing, where he teaches courses on instructional strategies, educational technology, and computer-aided instruction. His PhD is in curriculum and instruction.